MIPLC Studies

Edited by

Prof. Dr. Christoph Ann, LL.M. (Duke Univ.)
Technische Universität München

Prof. Robert Brauneis
The George Washington University Law School

Prof. Dr. Josef Drexl, LL.M. (Berkeley)
Max-Planck-Institut für Innovation und Wettbewerb

Prof. Dr. Michael Kort, University of Augsburg

Prof. Dr. Thomas M.J. Möllers
University of Augsburg

Prof. Dr. Dres. h.c. Joseph Straus,
Max Planck Institute for Intellectual Property and Competition Law

Volume 21

Nuno de Araújo Sousa e Silva

The Ownership Problems of Overlaps in European Intellectual Property

 Nomos MIPLC Munich Intellectual Property Law Center   Augsburg München Washington DC

Die Deutsche Nationalbibliothek verzeichnet diese Publikation in
der Deutschen Nationalbibliografie; detaillierte bibliografische
Daten sind im Internet über http://dnb.d-nb.de abrufbar.

The Deutsche Nationalbibliothek lists this publication in the Deutsche
Nationalbibliografie; detailed bibliographic data is available
in the Internet at http://dnb.d-nb.de .

a.t.: Munich, Munich Intellectual Property Law Center, Thesis "Master of Laws
in Intellectual Property and Competion Law (LL.M. IP)", 2013

ISBN 978-3-8487-1395-0

1. Auflage 2014
© Nomos Verlagsgesellschaft, Baden-Baden 2014. Printed in Germany. Alle Rechte, auch
die des Nachdrucks von Auszügen, der fotomechanischen Wiedergabe und der Übersetzung, vorbehalten. Gedruckt auf alterungsbeständigem Papier.

This work is subject to copyright. All rights are reserved, whether the whole or part of
the material is concerned, specifically those of translation, reprinting, re-use of illustrations, broadcasting, reproduction by photocopying machine or similar means, and
storage in data banks. Under § 54 of the German Copyright Law where copies are made
for other than private use a fee is payable to »Verwertungsgesellschaft Wort«, Munich.

Aos meus avós:

José e Cândida

Joaquim e Lurdes

Foreword

This small book is the result of a Master thesis written between July and early September 2013, minor corrections and updates having been made. Intellectual Property is indeed a fascinating subject, though an ever-changing one. It is my faint hope that the fundamental thoughts expressed here can still bear some validity and interest in the upcoming years. I would be glad to get any comments, suggestions or ideas by mail (nsousaesilva@gmail.com).

In the process of writing this thesis I have thoroughly benefited from the physical and human resources of the MIPLC. I am deeply indebted to all the people that with small or big comments and conversations have expanded my knowledge and perspectives on this and many other topics, not only related to Intellectual Property. I must specially mention Domink Niedersüss for his meticulous reading of my thesis followed by the proverbial G and T and the "three cool cats": Paraskevi, Kothainaiki and Kalliopi.

I am also obliged to Professor Matthias Leistner for his careful, precious and ready guidance. I owe gratitude to my aunt Julie and uncle Luis Miguel for the generosity of an attentive reading of the final text.

I remain thankful to my parents in every breath I take.

Finally, I want to thank Rita for showing me that "like billowing clouds, like the incessant gurgle of the brook, the longing of the spirit can never be stilled" (Hildegard von Bingen).

Vila Nova de Gaia, 9th March 2014

Inhaltsverzeichnis

Acronyms and Abbreviations	11
Abstract	15
I – The legal framework of ownership and overlaps	17
A. Introduction: the problem	17
1. The phenomenon of overlaps	17
2. Why are split ownerships a problem?	22
3. Methodology	26
4. Sequence	28
B. The ownership of copyright	29
1. Author's rights vs. copyright	30
2. Special cases of ownership	32
a) Employee's creations	33
1. Work for hire	33
2. Presumed assignment or licence	34
b) Several authors	35
1. Joint Works	35
2. Connected works	36
3. Collective works	37
4. Copyright in cinematographic works	38
II – Cases of ownership problems of overlaps	40
A. The case of trade marks & designs	40
B. The case of trade marks & copyright	45
C. The case of registered designs & copyright	50
D. The case of databases: sui generis right & copyright	56
E. The case of software and computer implemented inventions	61
III – Possible solutions to the problem	65
A. The extent of the problem	65

Inhaltsverzeichnis

    B. A general solution?   66
        1. Avoiding the problem   66
           a) Avoiding overlaps?   66
           b) Avoiding differences in ownership?   68
        2. Prevalence   68
        3. Contractual or quasi-contractual solutions   69
           a) Implied licence   69
           b) Abuse of rights   71
        4. Expanding copyright-internal solutions by analogy   72
           a) On Analogy   73
           b) Connected works   76
           c) Joint works   77

IV – Conclusion   79

Annex   81

Annex I: The interface of designs and copyright under Russian law   81

Annex II: Selected Legislative Provisions   84

Bibliography   105

Acronyms and Abbreviations

AIDA	Annali italiani del diritto d'autore, della cultura e dello spettacolo
AIPPI	International Association for the Protection of Industrial Property
art.	Article
BC	The Berne Convention for the Protection of Literary and Artistic Works
BoA	Board of Appeal of the OHIM
BGB	Bürgerliches Gesetzbuch (German Civil Code)
BGH	Bundesgerichtshof (German Federal Court of Justice)
CDPA	Copyright, Designs and Patents Act 1988 [United Kingdom]
CDR	Council Regulation (EC) No 6/2002 of 12 December 2001 on Community designs OJ L 3, 5.1.2002, p. 1–24
CPD	Directive 2009/24/EC of the European Parliament and of the Council of 23 April 2009 on the legal protection of computer programs (Codified version) OJ L 111, 5.5.2009 p.16–22
CJEU	Court of Justice of the European Union, formerly designated European Court of Justice.
CTM	Community Trade Mark
CTMR	Council Regulation (EC) No 207/2009 of 26 February 2009 on the Community trade mark (codified version) OJ L78, 24.3.2009, p. 1–42
CRD	Community Registered Design
DatD	Directive 96/9/EC of the European Parliament and of the Council of 11 March 1996 on the legal protection of databases OJ L077, 27.3.1996, p.20–28
ed	editor
edn	edition
EE	Edward Elgar
EIPR	European Intellectual Property Review

Acronyms and Abbreviations

EPC	Convention on the Grant of European Patents (European Patent Convention)
ERPL	European Review of Private Law
fn	footnote
GC	General Court, formerly designated Court of First Instance
GIs	Geographical Indications
GRUR	Gewerblicher Rechtsschutz und Urheberrecht
GRUR Int	Gewerblicher Rechtsschutz und Urheberrecht Internationaler Teil
HLR	Harvard Law Review
ICESCR	International Covenant on Economic, Social and Cultural Rights (adopted 3 January 1976) 993 UNTS 3
IIC	International Review of Intellectual Property and Competition Law
IP	Intellectual Property
IPQ	Intellectual Property Quarterly
IPRs	Intellectual Property Rights
JIPITEC	Journal of Intellectual Property, Information Technology and E-Commerce Law
JIPLP	Journal of Intellectual Property Law and Practice
JIPR	Journal of Intellectual Property Rights
JWIP	Journal of World Intellectual Property
JZ	Juristen Zeitung
ItalCA	Legge sul diritto d'autore, Legge 22.4.1941 n° 633, G.U. 16.7.1941 (Italian Copyright Act)
n	note
OHIM	Organization for the Harmonization of the Internal Market
OJLS	Oxford Journal of Legal Studies
OUP	Oxford University Press
ÖUrhG	Bundesgesetz über das Urheberrecht an Werken der Literatur und der Kunst und über verwandte Schutzrechte (Urheberrechtsgesetz) 1936 (Austrian Copyright Act)

Acronyms and Abbreviations

para(s)	paragraph(s)
PTCA	Código do Direito de Autor e dos Direitos Conexos, Decreto-Lei n.º 63/85, de 14 de Março (Portuguese Copyright Act)
RIDA	Revue Internationale du Droit d'Auteur
rn	randnummer
S	Section
TFEU	Consolidated version of Treaty on the Functioning of the European Union
TRIPS	Agreement on Trade-Related Aspects of Intellectual Property Rights, Marrakesh Agreement Establishing the World Trade Organization, Annex 1C
UNTS	United Nations Treaties Series
UrhG	Gesetz über Urheberrecht und verwandte Schutzrechte (Urheberrechtsgesetz) 1965 (German Copyright Act)
USC	The United States Code
WIPO	World Intellectual Property Organization
WIPR	World Intellectual Property Report
ZGE	Zeitschrift für Geistiges Eigentum
ZUM	Zeitschrift für Urheber- und Medienrecht
ZUM-RD	Zeitschrift für Urheber- und Medienrecht Rechstsprechungdienst

Abstract

Due to a variety of factors, Intellectual Property rights are expanding and, as a result, overlapping more than ever before. This phenomenon poses a wide array of problems and challenges to a system which was initially devised as comprising a set of isolated compartments, each with its defined purpose, object, and specific set of rules. As no careful thought on the interaction of these rights in cases of overlapping protection seems to have been given by the legislators yet, the solutions to the arising questions are far from obvious or established.

Among the diverging rules between IPRs the ones concerning ownership and entitlement can easily lead to situations where different rights on the same object are owned by different persons. Thus the question emerges: what happens when two (or more) different people own different rights whose object is the same? How to solve the situation where objective cumulation is not mirrored by subjective cumulation?

If a professor creates an original database and is accordingly entitled to copyright and, her employer, the University has put substantial investment in its creation, owning the *sui generis* right therein, how can exploitation occur? What rules regulate the conflict between the creator of a logo and the company that registers and uses it as a trade mark?

These questions are analysed under European law, focusing on the existing corpus of EU primary and secondary legislation and jurisprudence. When the EU body of law provides no guidance or a national example is required, that analysis focuses on three countries: Germany, France and the UK, other jurisdictions being also considered.

The paper starts by describing the occurrence of overlaps and the dangers deriving from split ownership. A study of the diverging rules of copyright ownership is necessary in order to define some operative concepts. The issue is then considered in five specific cases of overlapping protection: trade marks and designs, trade marks and copyright, designs and copyright, database *sui generis* right and copyright and, finally, copyright and patents in the field of computer programs.

From the analysis of these cases some conclusion are drawn regarding the way legal rules answer to the split ownership problem and to what extent the existing approach is commendable.

Abstract

The paper ponders and suggests some solutions to the problem, namely the convergence of ownership rules, the avoidance of overlaps *tout court*, the prevalence of the closest regime, abuse of rights, implied licences, and expanding copyright solutions by analogy. It is suggested that the latter is the best approach even though a combination of some of the mechanisms described is to be expected. It concludes by considering possible legislative intervention and the form it might take.

I – The legal framework of ownership and overlaps

A. Introduction: the problem

1. The phenomenon of overlaps

When we look at a product we seldom realise the wide range of intangible goods it often embodies.[1] The design of the product, defining its appearance, may also be seen as an indication of origin (shape trade mark); its logo may be a work protected by copyright but can constitute a trade mark as well; additionally, some of the functional features of the product may be protected by patents (or utility models/petty patents).[2] Thus several underlying intangible goods coexist in that single product: its aesthetic appearance, its ability to indicate an origin and its functionality.

Furthermore, the same intangible achievement might be protected by more than a single Intellectual Property right. For example, goodwill[3] – an intangible good – might be protected simultaneously by trade mark and design laws. It is true that one of the purposes of trade mark law is to protect

---

1 On the notion of intangible goods (*immaterialgüter*) and Intellectual Property in general see N P de Carvalho, 'Towards a Unified Theory of Intellectual Property: The Differentiating Capacity (and Function) as the Thread That Unites All its Components' [2012] JWIP 251; A Rahmatian, 'Intellectual Property and the Concept of Dematerialised Property in S Bright (ed) *Modern Studies in Property Law* vol 6 (Hart Publishing 2011) 361; H-P Götting, 'Der Begriff des Geistigen Eigentums' [2005] GRUR 353; A Ohly, 'Geistiges Eigentum?' [2003] JZ 545.
2 A Kur, 'Cumulation of IP Rights Pertaining to Product Shapes. An "Illegitimate Offspring" of IP Law?' in G Ghidini and L Genovesi (eds), *Intellectual Property and Market Power* (Eudeba 2008) 613, 614.
3 Defined classically as "the attractive force that brings in custom" *e I.R.C. v Muller & Co's Margarine Ltd.* [1901] A.C. 217, 224, per Lord Macnaghten. On the notion *see* B E Cookson, 'The significance of goodwill' EIPR [1991] 248.

I – The legal framework of ownership and overlaps

goodwill in a certain sign[4] whilst the protection dispensed by design law to that intangible good (goodwill) is only a consequence of the protection of another intangible good: the aesthetic appearance.[5] In fact, almost all IP rights protect more than one intangible good, even though they are devised with a function, an objective. They aim to protect a certain achievement or investment. As stated in CJEU's jurisprudence, developed mainly in the field of exhaustion, each IP right has its *specific subject matter*.[6]

When two IP rights protect the same "manifestation", be it a computer program,[7] an original database or the shape of a product, this results in the so-called overlapping protection of Intellectual Property rights, also called objective cumulation (cumulation regarding the same object).

---

4 In most recent times the CJEU has simultaneously recognized several functions to trade marks and established an additional requirement for infringement: the adverse affection of a protected function of the trade mark. The functions mentioned by the Court in an apparently non-exhaustive list are "not only the essential function of the trade mark, which is to guarantee to consumers the origin of the goods or services, but also its other functions, in particular that of guaranteeing the quality of the goods or services in question and those of communication, investment or advertising" (Case C-487/07 *L'Oréal v Bellure* [2009] ETMR 55 para 58). On the origins of the theory *see* T Cohen Jehoram, 'The Function Theory in European Trade Mark Law and the Holistic Approach of the CJEU' (2012) 102 The Trademark Reporter 1243.

5 With a similar analysis cf G Dinwoodie, 'Trademark And Copyright: Complements or Competitors?' in J Ginsburg and J Besek (eds), *Adjuncts and Alternatives to Copyright* (ALAI-USA 2002) 506, 518.

6 Case 78/70 *Deutsche Grammophon* [1971] ECR 487 para 11. This notion has been criticised as illogical and wrong C G Miller, 'Magill: Time to abandon the "specific subject matter" concept' [1993] EIPR 415. To our purposes it is just another way of highlighting that each Intellectual Property Right has function(s) that explain its form. Making that analysis in the context of trade mark law see I S Fhima, 'How Does 'Essential Function' Doctrine Drive European Trade Mark Law?' [2005] IIC 401.

7 Which can be decomposed in two different realities: software, protected by copyright and a computer implemented invention, protected by patents.

A. Introduction: the problem

This phenomenon of overlaps,[8] i.e. the co-existence of different exclusive rights whose object is the same, occurs more and more as a result of the expansion of intellectual property[9] and poses a whole range of problems.[10]

The term **"object"** is used here to signify the manifestation that will attract protection. In the case of overlaps the object of the converging rights is the same although the intangible **subject matter** is normally different. For instance in the case of databases, copyright protects the expression, i.e. the original arrangement, whereas the *sui generis* right will protect the investment put into the creation of such a database. The same happens with a logo that attracts both copyright and trade mark protection. The logo is the object, while the subject matter for copyright is the original expression (the work) and for trade mark law it is the sign indicating commercial origin. Object is

---

8   Also referred to as cumulation or concurrence, T Cohen Jehoram et al, *European Trademark Law* (Kluwer Law 2010) 555. On the several understandings of convergence cf G Dinwoodie, 'Concurrence and Convergence of Rights: The concerns of the US Supreme Court in Intellectual Property Law' in W Grosheide and J Brinkhof (eds), *Articles on Crossing Borders between traditional and actual Intellectual Property Law* (Intersentia 2004) 5-12.

9   R Moufang, 'The interface between patents and plant variety rights in Europe' (WIPO-UPOV/SYM/03/06) 4; A Kur and H Grosse Ruse–Khan, 'Enough is Enough – The Notion of Binding Ceilings in International Intellectual Property Protection' (2008) Max Planck Institute for Intellectual Property, Competition & Tax Law Research Paper Series No. 09-01, 8 <http://ssrn.com/abstract=1326429> accessed 16 August 2013 ("…until now, the development of international IP protection has been a one-way route – once rights have been inscribed into the text of an IP convention, they basically become sacrosanct for now and the future. Revision conferences (with only a few remarkable exceptions) have regularly served the purpose of further strengthening the position of right holders; hardly ever was an effort undertaken to question or curtail incumbent rules"). G Dinwoodie, 'Trademark and copyright' (n 5) 504 also points out the practical relevance of opportunistic litigation; A Quaedvlieg, 'Concurrence and Convergence in Industrial Design: 3-Dimensional Shapes Excluded by Trademark Law' in W Grosheide and J Brinkhof (eds), *Articles on Crossing Borders* (n 8) 23, 25 speaks of an "osmosis between the formerly separated terrains of technical subject-matter, marketing and culture".

10 Some recent literature addressing these is N Wilkof and S Basheer (eds), *Overlapping Intellectual Property Rights* (OUP 2012); E Derclaye and M Leistner, *Intellectual Property Overlaps* (Hart Pub 2011); R Tomkowicz, *Intellectual Property Overlaps* (Routledge 2011).

also to be distinguished from **"product"**, the item sold as a unit in the marketplace (a single economic object).[11-12]

The criterion to determine what constitutes an **object** should be taken from an economic perspective. An object is what is economically seen as a unit, something which cannot be exploited separately.[13] Accordingly, if a product has a functional aspect protected by patents and also bears a trade mark, it is clear that both the trade mark and the patent can be exploited independently, since they have different objects. Hence, there is no overlap. On the other hand, if a logo is simultaneously protected by trade mark and copyright there is no way in which one can exploit it without having cleared both rights. The object of the IPRs is the same, so an overlap occurs.

These overlaps have the potential to challenge freedom of competition, freedom of expression and the arts, and free movement of goods by curtailing the use of exceptions, affecting the balance achieved within a certain exclusive right.[14] Another matter of concern is "rejuvenation". By using several

---

11 Expression of F Macrez, 'Cumuls de Droits Intellectuels sur les créations informatiques' in A Cruquenaire and S Dusollier (eds), *Le Cumul des Droits Intellectuels* (Larcier 2009) 87. Unless otherwise noted, all translations found throughout the text are the author's.

12 In the same vein *see* A Kur, 'Cumulation of IPRs' (n 2) 615. These notions and terminologies are, however, far from established. For instance when addressing the notion of *cumul*, J-C Galloux, 'Des possibles cumuls de protection par les droits de propriété intellectuelle' in *L'entreprise face à la contrefaçon des droits de propriété intellectuelle* (Litec 2002) 81, submits that the expression should be reserved for those situations in which "two or more rights, of a different nature, exist together in the same physical object while having partially or totally the same legal subject-matter" (*objet juridique*). He nonetheless distinguishes *cumul* from coexistence on the basis of physical separability (at 82) and concludes that coexistence cases are not problematic. E Derclaye and M Leistner (n 10) 3-5 also adopt a slightly different approach. On the different notions *see* O-A Rognstad, 'The multiplicity of territorial IP rights and its impact on competition' in J Rosén (ed) *Individualism and Collectiveness in Intellectual Property Law* (EE 2012) 55 fn1 (with further references).

13 This is a similar reasoning to the German limits on fragmentation through licencing according to which a licence is not valid unless it encompasses a unity that makes economic and technical sense. The object of the licence must be capable of being exploited by itself (BGH [1992] GRUR 310 *Taschenbuch-Lizenz*; T Dreier and G Schulze, *UrhG Kommentar* (4th edn, C.H. Beck 2013) § 31 rn9).

14 A Kur, 'Exceptions to Protection Where Copyright and Trade Mark Overlap' in J Ginsburg and J Besek (eds), *Adjuncts and Alternatives* (n 5) 594; see also M Senftleben, 'Overprotection and Protection Overlaps in Intellectual Property Law – the Need for Horizontal Fair Use Defences' in A Kur and V Mizaras (eds), *The Structure of Intellectual Property Law: Can One Size Fit All?* (EE 2011).

A. Introduction: the problem

forms of protection, some of which are very long lasting (copyright's duration in the EU is now 70 years after the death of the author)[15] or even potentially "eternal", like trade marks, a right holder can frustrate the purpose of a limited term of protection[16] in systems such as patents, designs, and, to a lesser extent, copyright.[17-18]

The specific overlap problem I've chosen to tackle in this paper relates to ownership. What happens when two (or more) different people own different

---

15 The term has been harmonized in the EU by the Term Directive in 1993, amended in 2001, codified in 2006 in the form of Directive 2006/116/EC of the European Parliament and of the Council of 12 December 2006 on the term of protection of copyright and certain related rights (codified version) [2006] OJ L372/12 (**Term Directive**) and extended by Directive 2011/77/EU of the European Parliament and of the Council of 27 September 2011 amending Directive 2006/116/EC on the term of protection of copyright and certain related rights [2011] OJ L265/1. Despite the multiple legislative interventions, harmonization has not been totally successful as demonstrated by C Angelopoulos, 'The Myth of European Term Harmonisation: 27 Public Domains for the 27 Member States' [2012] IIC 567.

16 G Ghidini, 'From here to eternity? On the overlap of shape trade marks with design protection' in J Drexl, R Hilty, L Boy and C Godt (eds), *Technology and Competition. Contributions in Honour of Hanns Ullrich* 55 ff. (concluding against the overlap between trade marks and designs at 66).

17 Of course this problem must be equated with the scope of protection granted by each of these IP rights, which is not exactly the same. The protection granted by copyright is directed only against copying and limited to a certain expression, whereas the strength of patent protection is far superior. Save for trade marks with a reputation, its protection is limited by the principle of speciality.

18 This is to be distinguished from the situation of "appropriation of the public domain" (works whose copyright has expired) by registering as a trade mark works such as the painting Monalisa (refused in Germany on the ground of lack of distinctive character, see [1998] GRUR 1021). In that situation the work belongs to nobody (or everybody depending on how to regard the public domain). On the topic *see* J Jankowski, *Markenschutz für Kunstwerke* (Nomos 2012) (concluding that there is no need for an absolute ground of refusal to protect the public domain) and M Senftleben, 'Der Kulturelle Imperativ des Urheberrechts' in M Weller, N Kemle, T Dreier and M Lynen (eds), *Kunst im Markt – Kunst im Recht* (Nomos 2010) 75 ff. In favour of introducing an absolute ground of refusal for such situation with an exception for those who were already exploiting the work as a trade mark before it went into the public domain *see* A Wandtke and W Bullinger, 'Die Marke als urheberrechtlich schutzfähiges Werk' [1997] GRUR 573, 578. Rejecting such idea and allowing the trade mark see the recent decision by the BGH [2012] GRUR 612 *Medusa*.

rights whose object is the same? How should we approach a situation where objective cumulation is not mirrored by subjective cumulation?[19]

The following considerations assume that there are no express contractual provisions dealing with ownership issues. [20]

2. Why are split ownerships a problem?

The phenomenon of overlapping rights with different owners (split ownership) occurs systematically in relation to copyright and neighbouring rights. It is part of a wider aspect of modern copyright known as fragmentation.[21] If A records B singing a song composed by C (actually, music by C and lyrics by D), and a third party wants to explore the recording: (s)he will have to gather licences from all these people, unless A has already done so and his licence allows sub-licensing.

The combined efforts of the copyright legislator and the market forces have generated mechanisms to deal with the fragmentation phenomenon such as collective management organizations,[22] the connected works doctrine, deemed authorship in movies[23] and compulsory licensing.[24] Furthermore, market participants are also cognisant of the necessities generated by fragmentation and act accordingly, mainly through contract.

---

19 F Verkade, 'The cumulative Effect of Copyright Law and Trademark Law: Which takes precedence?' in J Kabel and G Mom (eds) Intellectual Property and Information Law: Essays in Honour of Herman Cohen Jehoram (Kluwer Law 1998) 69, 70.
20 A brief and practical approach to contracts regulating ownership can be found in T Golder and A Mayer, 'Whose IP is it anyway?' [2009] JIPLP 165.
21 Fragmentation covers both layers of rights (copyright + neighbouring rights), multiple sub-rights (e.g. reproduction and making available) or fields of use (broadcasting, online transmission, performance, etc.). This is also referred to as "atomisation". Discussing it see 'Note: A justification for allowing fragmentation in copyright' [2011] HLR 1751.
22 For an overview *see* D Gervais (ed), *Collective Management of Copyright and Related Rights* (2nd edn, Kluwer 2010).
23 See below **I.B.2.b) 4.**
24 E.g. arts. 9 and 10 Council Directive 93/83EEC of 27 September 1993 on the coordination of certain rules concerning copyright and rights related to copyright applicable to satellite broadcasting and cable retransmission (**satellite and cable directive**). This often means granting a remuneration right instead of a property right. M Ricolfi, Collective Rights Management in a Digital Environment in G Ghidini and L Genovesi (eds) (n 2) 383, 388 argues that collecting societies have the effect of shifting copyright from property to liability.

A. Introduction: the problem

In the case of overlaps involving different IPRs there is no collective management in place[25] and market participants seem to be less aware of the problem. This can lead to a tragedy of the anticommons. As defined by Heller: "In an anticommons (...) multiple owners are each endowed with the right to exclude others from a scarce resource, and no one has an effective privilege of use. When there are too many owners holding rights of exclusion, the resource is prone to under use – *a tragedy of the anticommons.*"[26] One example presented by the Author was found in post-socialist economies. In the transition – "from Marx to markets" – there was a fragmentation of rights in Moscow's storefronts, multiple rights to the same property were distributed amongst several stakeholders.[27] Thus, a person interested in using a shop would need to collect all rights in order to operate. These high transaction costs explained the empty stores in Moscow, an underuse.[28] In a later article, with Rebeca Eisenberg,[29] Heller makes the same analysis regarding biomedical research and upstream patents, preventing downstream innovation.

It can be counter-argued that blocking effects are not a real problem. After all, IPRs are granted to protect the interests of the owner because society believes they merit protection. To borrow the example given by Peter Prescott QC in *Griggs v Ross Evans*,[30] an artist approaches a bank with a proposal for a new logo. "If the bank started to use the artist's version of the logo after all, without his permission, they would be taking advantage of his skill and labour in coming up with the original design. Copyright law prohibits this. But if the artist were to sell his logo to a rival bank and that bank started to use his logo in connection with its business, that would be a misuse

---

25 Still, some solutions (in the field of patent law) such as clearinghouses and patent pools have emerged (not without problems of their own). On these see G V Overwalle, 'Individualism, collectivism and openness in patent law: from exclusion to inclusion through licensing' in J Rosén (n) 71.
26 M Heller,'The tragedy of the anticommons: property in the transition from Marx to markets' [1998] HLR 621.
27 Ibid 633 ff.
28 Ibid 639 ff.
29 'Can Patents Deter Innovation? The Anticommons in Biomedical Research' Science 280 (1998) 698 ("...privatization can go astray when too many owners hold rights in previous discoveries that constitute obstacles to future research"); see also M Heller, *The Gridlock Economy: How Too Much Ownership Wrecks Markets, Stops Innovation, and Costs Lives* (Basic Books 2010).
30 [2003] EWHC 2914 [26].

I – The legal framework of ownership and overlaps

of the business goodwill associated with the [sign]. Trademark law prohibits this."[31] These rights are negative rights, rights to control the activity of others[32] and requiring several layers of authorization is one way to regulate potential conflicts and to force understandings. One related example of this regulatory use of negative rights is present in the discussions regarding indigenous heritage protection.[33] A solution found in the trade mark statute of New Zealand of 2002, is to grant the right to control the use of Māori or aboriginal symbols by establishing an absolute ground of refusal if a trade mark's "use or registration would be likely to offend a significant section of the Community, including Māori".[34]

Additionally, it can be said, as it is happens with dependent patents,[35] that market forces will lead to an understanding and cross-licensing is likely to occur in case it is of interest for both owners to exploit the same object commercially.[36] However, even then, the problem is not solved at its root, its extension is limited but the potential for conflict is still there. Furthermore, unlike in most cases of patent dependency[37] and other follow-on innovation,

---

31 Ibid [27].
32 W Cornish, D Llewlyn and T Aplin, *Intellectual Property: Patents, Copyright, Trade Marks and Allied Rights* (7th edn, Sweet & Maxwell 2010) 7. It is debated e.g. in the plain packaging dispute, whether TRIPS grants a positive right to use to the trade mark owner (*see* T Voon and A Mitchell, 'Implications of WTO Law for Plain Packaging of Tobacco Products' in A. Mitchell, T. Voon and J. Liberman (eds), *Public Health and Plain Packaging of Cigarettes: Legal Issues* (EE 2012) 109, 115). The same is disputed in face of the text of art. 19 CDR (O Ruhl, *Gemeinshcafts-geschamcksmuster Kommentar* (2nd edn, Carl Heymanns 2010) 375). If that is affirmed some of our cases can be framed as a collision of rights and a contradiction in the system (antinomy). This would generate a lacuna due to collision.
33 For an overview see S V Lewinski (ed), *Intellectual Property & Indigenous Heritage* (2nd edn, Kluwer 2008).
34 Art. 17(1)(b)(ii). For a brief analysis see D Zografos, 'Tradition v Trade marks: The New Zealand Trade Marks Act 2002' in W Grosheide and J Brinkhof (eds), *Articles on Crossing Borders* (n 8) 279.
35 Also called overlapping patents. Analysing its occurrence see A Christie and C Dent, 'Non-overlapping rights: a patent misconception' [2010] EIPR 58.
36 C Shapiro, 'Navigating the Patent Thicket: Cross Licenses, Patent Pools, and Standard-Setting' in A Jaffe, J Lerner and S Stern (eds), *Innovation Policy and the Economy* vol 1 (MIT Press 2001) 119.
37 Addressing the problem in the field of biotechnology see e.g. recital 25 and art. 12 of Directive 98/44/EC of 6 July 1998 on the legal protection of biotechnological inventions OJ L213.

A. Introduction: the problem

there will not always be a mutual interest to exploit the object of the different rights independently.

Although the ownership problem of overlaps has affinities with the one of patent thickets, the origins of these different ownerships in overlaps will very often lie in one single set of events. Thus the relation between the different owners plays an essential role in the analysis. It is, nonetheless possible that two different rights overlap in the same object in spite of their holders being independent and unrelated. This will be the case when a software engineer writes code for a certain program without making a novelty-destroying disclosure and, later on, this technical solution is patented by a third party who independently reached that same solution.[38] This is a different situation from the one described *supra* in the *Griggs v Evans* hypothetical.[39] It is necessary to distinguish situations of "independent creation", where no copyright violation takes place from the remainder. In the former the existence of copyright is irrelevant as it produces no blocking effect.[40]

In an excellent article, Alexander Peukert identifies five subcategories of multiple rights or owners:[41]

– "Double invention and parallel trade marks", addressed mainly by rules such as first to file[42] and prior user rights;[43]
– "Unilateral combinations/adaptation of protected subject matter", whose solution is mainly to limit exclusivity;[44]
– "Group innovation/creativity concerning several rights", where solutions favouring concentration or joint exploitation are mentioned;[45]

---

38 When it comes to patent law it will be hard to make generalisations as much will depend on the drafting of each particular claim.
39 n 30 and accompanying text.
40 This results from the subjective notion of originality (see A Waisman, 'May authorship go objective?' [2009] JIPLP 583, 584).
41 'Individual multiple and collective ownership of intellectual property rights – which impact on exclusivitiy?' in A Kur and V Mizaras (eds) (n 14) 195, 200.
42 In Europe, art. 60(2) EPC for patents and arts. 6 and 8 CTMR for trademarks. The case of designs is more complex, involving registered and unregistered designs. For the former cf arts. 1(2)(b) and 25(1)(d) CDR. After 16 March of 2013 with the America Invents Act, US patent law abandoned the "first-to-invent" rule.
43 V.g § 12 PatGesetz (see R Kraßer, *Patentrecht* (6th edn, C.H.Beck 2009) 819 ff). Art. 28 of the Agreement on a Unified Patent Court deems national laws on prior user rights applicable to the European Patent with a unitary effect.
44 A Peukert (n 41) 203-207.
45 Ibid 207-208.

- "Parallel territorial rights", relating both to territoriality and its exceptions and addressed by doctrines such as exhaustion and by the rules of jurisdiction and conflict of laws;[46] and
- "Cumulation of different IPRs"

The last one is the subject of this study.[47] According to the same Author:[48] "This situation entails unique difficulties (...) [and] can only be resolved by applying a 'horizontal approach in search of overarching, general principles that form the basis of all IP rights".

3. Methodology

The international IP system does not provide much guidance on how overlaps should be regulated.[49] Furthermore, the issue of ownership of Intellectual Property in general and copyright in particular is so contentious that it has rarely been touched upon by the numerous multilateral treaties concerning IP.[50] It is a controversial question, whether or not indirect regulation, through a rule of conflicts of law, can be found in art. 5 BC.[51] In any case

---

46 Ibid 209-211. The challenges to territoriality are not only caused by the Internet but also by the wider phenomenon of globalisation (G Dinwoodie, 'Trademarks and Territory: Detaching Trademark Law from the Nation-State' (2004) 41 Houston Law Review 886).

47 As J-C Galloux (n 12) 81 notes there are also possibilities for overlaps between IP rights and rights of other nature (such as the conflict of personality rights and copyright or physical and intellectual property). These will not be addressed. I will neither cover the related problem of having different choice of law rules in overlapping IPRs mentioned by A Ohly, 'Choice of Law in the Digital Environment – Problems and Possible Solutions' in J Drexl and A Kur (eds) *Intellectual Property and Private International Law* (Hart Publishing 2005) 241, 249-250.

48 (n 41) 208-209.

49 E Derclaye and M Leistner (n 10) 24.

50 P Goldstein and B Hugenholtz, *International Copyright: Principles, Law, and Practice* (2nd edn, OUP 2010) 245.

51 See S Ricketson and J Ginsburg, *International Copyright and Neighbouring Rights* vol 2 (2nd edn, OUP 2006) 1292-1327 (at 1315 "The BC affords insufficient guidance as to the law applicable (...) to designation of initial copyright ownership and authorship status"); P Torremans, 'Choice of law in EU copyright directives' in E Derclaye (ed), *Research Handbook on the Future of EU Copyright* (EE 2009) 457-479 (stating "Whilst there is therefore no real choice of law rule in the Berne Convention it does seem to push Member States downs the road of the law of the protecting country").

A. Introduction: the problem

the international system of treaties and conventions is dependent on further action by national legislators.[52] When it comes to the European Union,[53] there's a supranational IP system in place that comprises EU-wide (unitary) trade marks,[54] designs,[55] plant varieties,[56] and geographical indications,[57] besides a substantial number of harmonisation directives.[58] These systems of protection interact with national law mainly on the basis of coexistence,[59] which allow for the so-called vertical overlaps.[60]

The problem at hand will be analysed under European law, focusing on the existing corpus of EU primary and secondary legislation and jurisprudence. When the EU body of law provides no guidance or a national example is required, I will turn mainly to three jurisdictions: Germany, France and the UK, without prejudice of analysing solutions found elsewhere. Germany is chosen for it is the paradigm of a monistic[61] *droit d'auteur* system, France is the typical example of the dualist *droit d'auteur* regime and the UK is the copyright system's representative.

---

52 Although a few States recognize direct effect to some of its provisions.
53 Except for the Regulation on Supplementary Protection Certificates the countries of the European Economic Area (Switzerland, Iceland, Norway and Liechtenstein) are not part to the unitary systems although they harmonize their laws by means of the Directives (Annex XVII of the EEA Agreement).
54 Council Regulation (EC) No 207/2009 of 26 February 2009, hereinafter **CTMR**.
55 Council Regulation (EC) No 6/2002 of 12 December 2001, hereinafter **CDR**.
56 Council Regulation (EC) No 2100/94 of 27 July 2004 hereinafter **CPVR**.
57 Relating to foodstuffs and agricultural products: Council Regulation (EC) No 2006/510 of 20 March 2006, for wines Regulation (EC) No 479/2008 of the Council of 29 April 2008 and for spirit drinks Regulation (EC) No 110/2008 of the European Parliament and of the Council of 15 January 2008.
58 For a summary analysis of the current EU law on intellectual property see A Kur and T Dreier, *European Intellectual Property Law – Text, Cases & Materials* (EE 2013).
59 Recital 6 and art. 1(2) of the CTMR, Recital 31 and art. 96 of the CDR. When it comes to GIs, only the system set for foodstuffs is exclusive, the one for wines and spirits allows coexistence (DG Agriculture, "Background Paper to the Green Paper on Agricultural Product Quality" (2008) 4). The CPVR has established an exclusive regime (art. 1).
60 E Derclaye and M Leistner (n 10) 43.
61 In dualistic systems moral rights (as opposed to economic rights) are eternal and unassignable (e.g. L-121-1) whereas in a monistic system the economic rights and the moral rights have the same duration. Using Eugen Ulmer's famous metaphor (*Urheber- und Verlagsrecht* (3rd edn, Springer 1980) 116), in a monistic system economic and moral rights are seen as "two branches from the same tree".

This work will address mainly the interaction of copyright with other IPRs.[62] Due to its tendency to cumulate, copyright has been suggestively called the "promiscuous member of the IP village".[63] Additionally, the rules on ownership of copyright have hardly been touched upon by the EU legislature which renders this problem even more acute.

4. Sequence

Bearing in mind the controversial and non-harmonised nature of copyright-ownership rules and copyright's central role in overlaps it is convenient devote a whole section to the analysis of their specific regime and to the definition of some essential notions. This will also help us understand where the biggest potential for split ownerships lies and to seek inspiration for possible solutions.

Subsequently, I will turn to specific cases of overlaps (**II**). Five situations have been chosen. Due to the simplicity of the ownership rules, I will start by addressing the case of trademark and designs (**A**). Since it obeys essentially the same principles, the case of trademarks and copyright follows (**B**). To come full circle in the field of "product appearance" overlaps, the case of designs and copyright is examined (**C**). I will then turn to the case of copyright and the database maker's *sui generis* right (**D**), to conclude by studying the interface of copyrighted software and patented computer implemented inventions (**E**). Each of these sections ends with a summary.

From these cases I will draw some conclusions on existing rules and assess the extent of the problem, before proceeding to evaluate possible solutions based on existing law. I will conclude by assessing possible legislative intervention and the form it might take.

Two annexes are found at the end of the document: the first contains a brief analysis of the interface of copyright and designs under Russian law and the second provides the reader with a selection of legislative provisions cited in the text.

---

62 As until now there is not a unitary copyright in the EU, this constitutes a "mixed overlap" (different rights with different territorial scope); E Derclaye and M Leistner (n 10) 32.

63 A Quaedvlieg, 'Overlap/relationships between copyright and other intellectual property rights' in E Derclaye (ed), *Research handbook* (n 51) 480, 483.

B. The ownership of copyright

As William Cornish[64] puts it: "Throughout the history of intellectual property there has been a fundamental tension between the creator (inventor, author) – whose activity is the key to entitlement – and the investor/entrepreneur – who needs the right in order to turn the subject-matter to commercial account, potentially for the benefit of both...".

In the field of patent law the solution tends to be alike: the invention belongs to the inventor[65] unless the inventive activity takes place in the course of his work.[66] In that case, the invention usually belongs to the employer.[67] The inventive activity might be eligible for additional remuneration, according to national regulations. The detail of these regulations ranges from the minimalist Portuguese solution: a general statement "if the inventive activity is not specially considered in the payment, the inventor has the right to be remunerated according to the importance of the invention"[68] to the very detailed German Act on employer's inventions (*Arbeitnehmererfindugsgesetz*).[69]

When it comes to copyright ownership there is a rather bigger divide.

---

64 'The expansion of Intellectual Property Rights' in Schricker, Dreier and Kur (eds) *Geistiges Eigentum im Dienst der Innovation* (Nomos 2001) 9,16.
65 There are, of course, problems of "inventorship", determining if a certain contribution is important/inventive enough for its responsible to be deemed co-inventor.
66 Art. 60 EPC limits itself to determine the applicable law. Hess in R Hacon and J Pagenberg (eds), *Concise European Patent Law* (2 edn, Wolters Kluwer 2009) 64.
67 E.g. S39 of the UK Patents Act of 1977. The situation in Germany is more complex. See S Wolk, 'Remuneration of Employee Inventors – Is there a Common European Ground? A comparison of National laws on Compensation of Inventors in Germany, France, Spain, Sweden and the United Kingdom' [2011] IIC 272; S Wolk, 'EU Intellectual Property Law and Ownership in Employment Relationships' in *Information & Communication Technology, Legal Issues, Scandinavian Studies in Law* (Wahlgren 2010) 419.
68 Art. 59(2) of the Portuguese Industrial Property Code, providing for a dispute resolution system in case an agreement is not reached on the amount to be paid.
69 For a thorough analysis and an annex with a translation of the law *see* M Trimborn, *Employees Inventions in Germany: A Handbook for International Business* (Wolters Kluwer 2009). Concerning the situation in the UK *see* J Pila, 'Sewing the Fly Buttons on the Statute' Employee Inventions and the Employment Context' 32 (2012) OJLS 265; W Cornish, D Llewely and T Aplin (n 32) 291 ff. With a French and comparative perspective see J-P Martin, *Droit des inventions de salariés* (3rd edn Lexis Nexis 2005).

I – The legal framework of ownership and overlaps

1. Author's rights vs. copyright

Copyright laws follow one of two big systems: author's rights (*droit d'auteur*), prevailing in the civil law tradition, based on the personal relation between the creator and the work and the Anglo-American copyright system, which takes a more economic, incentive-based, approach.[70]

One of the major manifestations of the different philosophical underpinnings of these systems is the issue of ownership of rights, specifically whether companies can be initial owners of copyright. While the *droit d'auteur* systems (such as France,[71] Germany,[72] and most civil law countries) regard the author as a natural person (a perspective which is also found in some international treaties, like art. 15 ICESCR[73] and arguably the Berne Convention),[74] the copyright systems (notably the US[75] and the UK,[76] by means of the 'work for hire' doctrine) have no issue with copyright being

---

70 For a nice overview of the differences see S V Lewinski, *International Copyright Law and Policy* (OUP 2008) 33 ff.; J Ginsburg, 'A Tale of Two Copyrights: Literary Property in Revolutionary France and America' [1990] Tulane Law Review 991 (demonstrating that there was more in common, both in theory and in practice, between the early French and American copyright statutes than what is normally conveyed); A Strowel, *Droit d'auteur et copyright* (Brulyant 1993).
71 Lucas and Lucas, *Traité de la propriété littéraire et artistique* (4th edn, Lexis Nexis 2012) 155-156 (noting that this also seems to result from Infopaq's criterion, as only natural persons are capable of an intellectual creation).
72 § 7 UrhG.
73 UN Committee on Economic, Social and Cultural Rights (CESCR), *General Comment No. 17: The Right of Everyone to Benefit from the Protection of the Moral and Material Interests Resulting from any Scientific, Literary or Artistic Production of Which He or She is the Author (Art. 15, Para. 1 (c) of the Covenant)* (12 January 2006) E/C.12/GC/17, 3 available at: <http://www.refworld.org/docid/441543594.html> accessed 24 August 2013.
74 S V Lewinski (n 70) 129 (arguing that "all means of interpretation result in (…) only natural persons are authors in the meaning of the Convention"); A Dietz, 'The Concept of Author under the Berne Convention' 155 (1993) RIDA 2, 26 (with the same conclusion and stating that "the assertion that the simple replacement of employed authors by employers and other producers is permissible under the Convention is extremely questionable").
75 17 USC § 101 and § 201(b).
76 S 11(2) CDPA.

vested in legal persons *ab initio* and employ the term "author" indiscriminately.[77]

There are also countries of a *droit d'auteur* tradition that allow, in specific situations, for copyright to be vested originally in legal persons.[78] This exception is justified mainly in situations where the dispersion/fragmentation that would otherwise be generated could render the exploitation of a work too impractical.[79] Countries like Portugal[80] or France[81] have provisions regarding collective works according to which the promoter of a collective project, often a legal person, might own the copyright in those creations.[82] Jurisdictions in this tradition have no problem with the transfer of copyright[83] to legal persons by means of a contract.[84]

Some other countries, such as Germany or Austria have no exceptions to the creator's principle (*Schöpferprinzip*).[85] In these countries, copyright can only be vested in natural persons and, accordingly, ownership is reserved to authors. This also implies that no contractual assignment can occur, copyright is non-transferrable, unless by inheritance.[86] However, even in the latter

---

77 According to J Sterling, *World Copyright law* (3rd edn, Sweet and Maxwell 2008) 1209 one has to distinguish between author in the strict sense ("the individual who by creative contribution produces a work") and in the broader sense (the one defined by law). He also believes the BC refers to an individual (at 207).

78 Which is not really synonymous with recognizing authorship; what happens is a detachment between authorship and ownership by operation of the law. A Dietz (n 74) 12.

79 P Goldstein and B Hugenholtz (n 50) 243.

80 Art 19 PTCA.

81 L 113-2(3) and L 113-5. On this rule in detail and in its wider context see the very well written article by P Gaudrat, 'Les démêlés intemporels d'un couple à succès: le créateur et l'investisseur' 190 (2001) RIDA 71-243 (specially 171 ff.), the Author considers this solution an "absolute irrationality" (at 193).

82 In a recent decision (22 March 2012, appeal no 11-10132) the French *Cour de cassation* held that this rule also covers moral rights.

83 In fact only the economic rights, as "...the core (moral) rights of the author (i.e. an individual) cannot be transferred" (A Strowel and B Vanbrabant, 'Copyright licensing: a European view' in J de Werra (ed) *Research Handbook on Intellectual Property Licensing* (EE 2013) 29, 34).

84 Arts. 13,14 CDADC; L-111-1; A Rahmatian, 'Dealing with rights in copyright-protected works: assignment and licences' in E Derclaye (ed), *Research handbook* (n 51) 286, 291 ("...the first assignment splits authorship from ownership").

85 § 7 UrhG; § 10 ÖUhrG; T Dreier and G Schulze (n 13) § 7 rn 1. On the topic see J Seignette, *Challenges to the creator doctrine* (Wolters Kluwer 1994).

86 § 29 UrhG; § 24(3) ÖUrhG.

cases there are provisions dealing with the problem of dispersion, such as the ones regulating copyright in films.[87]

2. Special cases of ownership

Due to its controversial nature, the EU has had a very modest intervention in matters of copyright ownership.[88] The existing approach is limited to the "technical copyright", in the Software and Database Directives and certain provisions in the Term Directive.[89]

Copyright remains to a large extent a national creature and in this respect, though the problems are common,[90] the differences are still marked. Within the EU there are only a few countries – like Ireland,[91] the UK or the Netherlands[92]– where the "work for hire" doctrine assigns the copyright originally to the employer. Nonetheless most Member States have specific provisions to deal with "problematic" cases of entitlement.

---

[87] § 88-94 UrhG; § 38, 39 ÖUrhG. For the situation under German law see Hartlieb and Schwarz, *Handbuch des Film-, Fernseh- und Videorechts* (5th edn, C.H.Beck 2011) 157 ff.

[88] Commission, 'Staff Working Paper on the Review of the EC Legal Framework in the field of copyright' SEC(2004)995, 14: "One of the reasons for the scarcity of international and Community rules governing the initial ownership is the sensitivity of the issue and the fact that it is so closely associated with the foundations of copyright and the objectives of the copyright regime in a given country." In C-518/08 *Salvador Dalí*, a case regarding *post-mortem* entitlement of the resale right, the CJEU confirmed that this is an issue for Member-States to determine.

[89] A Quaedvlieg, 'Authorship and Ownership: Authors, Entrepeneurs and Rights' in T-E Synodinou (ed), Codification of European Copyright Law (Kluwer Law 2012) 197, 207.

[90] A Metzger, 'Vom Einzelurheber zu Teams und Netzwerken: Erosion des Schöpferprinzips?' in S Leible, A Ohly and H Zech (eds), *Wissen – Markte – Geistiges Eigentum* 79 ff. (highlighting the challenges that networks and hierarchical structures pose to the principle).

[91] Section 23(1)(a) Ireland Copyright and Related Rights Act, 2000.

[92] Arts 7 and 8 Dutch Copyright Act, analysed by J Seignette, 'Authorship, Copyright Ownership and Works made on Commission and under Employment' in B Hugenholtz, A Quaedvlieg and D Visser (eds) *A Century of Dutch Copyright Law* (deLex 2012) 115.

B. The ownership of copyright

a) Employee's creations

1. Work for hire

Among the several copyright laws in the EU one can find specific solutions addressing employee's creations and the rights of employers. One approach is the aforementioned work for hire doctrine in the tradition of Anglo-American copyright law.[93] Pursuant to Section 11(2) of the UK CDPA: "Where a literary, dramatic, musical or artistic work or a film, is made by an employee in the course of his employment, his employer is the first owner of any copyright in the work subject to any agreement to the contrary". This provision creates a presumption of assignment. Unless there is an agreement to the contrary, the copyright will be vested in the employer, often a company. The usual point of controversy when applying this provision is whether the work was made in the course of employment.[94]

The equivalent provisions found in Dutch and Irish law have the same effect.[95] Unlike in the US,[96] in the EU "work for hire" type provisions do

---

93 For a critique of this doctrine see J Ginsbursg, 'The concept of authorship' (2002) 52 Depaul Law Review 1063, 1088-1092.
94 W Cornish, D Llewlyn and T Aplin (n 32) 531; J Seignette, (n 92) 129-134 (summarizing Dutch law and presenting a relevant number of factors to aid in the qualification).
95 Ns 91 and 92.
96 17 USC § 101 and § 201(b). The doctrine is however limited, the work must have been specifically commissioned, there must be a written agreement and the work must fall into one of the eligible categories (A Briges, 'Navigating the interface between utility patents and copyrights' in N Wilkof and S Basheer (eds) (n 10) 1, 11); A S Wernick, 'The work for hire and joint work copyright doctrines after CCNV V. REID: "What! You mean I don't own it even though I paid in full for it?"' (1990) 13 Hamline Law Review 287).

I – The legal framework of ownership and overlaps

not cover commissioned works.[97] These might, nonetheless, be a fertile ground for implied licences or even ownership in equity.[98]

2. Presumed assignment or licence[99]

In the context of labour contract or commissioned works most countries of the civil tradition understand that the author remains the owner of his work.[100] However, for some creations like software,[101] advertising, newspaper articles or photographs[102] there are different solutions in place. For instance French law has a presumption that the commissioned advertising

---

97 J Seignette 'Authorship' (n 92) 127 fn84 (Dutch law); R Clark, S Smyth and N Hall, *Intellectual Property in Ireland* (3rd edn, Bloomsbury 2010) 355; Laddie, Prescott and Vitoria, The modern law of copyright and designs, (4th edn, Lexis Nexis Butterworths 2011), vol I 946. The previous English law covered specific commissioned works like photographs. The current Portuguese law has a specific provision on photographs (art. 165 PTCA) according to which the copyright in that work is the commissioner's. That rule is also found e.g. in Italy (art. 88 ItalCA).
98 *Griggs v Evans* (n 30) [35] ("Now, it is often the case that a copyright work is commissioned by a client: the client pays for the work to be created, but nothing is said about copyright. It is clear that the free-lance artist is the legal owner of the copyright, for section 11 of the Act so provides. But who is the owner in equity?"); Laddie, Prescott and Vitoria, ibid, vol I 973-4 ("Ownership in equity can arise where the circumstances are such that the copyright, although belonging to the author at law, can properly be regarded as being held on trust by him for another person who is entitled to call for an assignment in order to perfect the legal title").
99 In this section I only address examples of statutory provisions. Implied licences (also in the employment context) and ownership in equity are considered below at **III.B.3**.
100 According to § 43 UrhG, unless a different result arises from the nature or content of the employer/commissioner relationship with the employee/commissioned, the former will not have any special treatment regarding exploitation rights (but can benefit from an implied licence (cf below n 333)). In a more restrictive vein cf. L-111-1 and art. 14 PTCA. There are also States, like Greece, which have an express provision establishing a general presumption of transfer of economic rights in the context of employment (limited to the fulfilment of the purpose of the contract) (art. 8 of the Greek Copyright Act).
101 Art. 2(3) of the Computer Programs Directive, for its analysis see **II.E**.
102 n 97.

work is licenced for that use[103] and professional journalist assign (by operation of the law) their copyright in newspaper articles.[104]

Another example found in some countries – and not only those which have copyright in official documents[105] – is a general presumption of assignment of copyright in favour of the State.[106]

b) Several authors

The area of works in which more than one original contribution is involved is a controversial one, "fraught with problems",[107] and the national solutions vary as does the terminology.[108] It is therefore convenient to present a small definition for each of the following terms – drawn from the comparison of national laws – and to briefly describe their treatment.

1. Joint Works

Works of joint authorship are those in which more than one person contributes to their final form.[109] Each author's contribution must be original, inseparable and indistinguishable in the final result.[110] Every contributor deemed an author will be entitled to copyright in the joint work;[111] hence

---

103 L-132-31.
104 L-132-36.
105 Art. 2(4) BC leaves it for Member States to decide. For instance, Portugal (arts. 7 and 9) and Italy (art. 5) deny it, whereas the Netherlands (art.11) and the UK (S 163-167) grant it.
106 As in Italy (art. 11) and in the UK (s11(2)).
107 D Marchese, 'Joint ownership of intellectual property' [1999] EIPR 364. See also the AIPPI summary report to question Q194 "The Impact of Co-Ownership of Intellectual Property Rights on their Exploitation" available at <https://www.aippi.org/download/commitees/194/SR194English.pdf> accessed 28 August 2013.
108 S Ricketson and J Ginsburg (n 51) vol I 363.
109 This is to be distinguished from a derivative work, which is a new work based on a prior existing one (E Ulmer (n 61) 190).
110 S10 CDPA (also *Ray v Classic FM Plc* [1998] ECC 488 [27]); § 8UrhG; art. 10 ItalCA; § 11(1) ÖUhrG. This is the so-called "strict approach" to joint authorship. Other countries do not require inseparability. For a comparison see M Walter in M Walter and S V Lewinski (eds), *European Copyright Law* (OUP 2010) 526 ff.
111 There are other cases of joint ownership, Laddie et al (n 97) vol I 964.

the permission of all authors is needed for a joint exploitation.[112] Since this unanimity rule is prone to create tensions among the joint authors, there are some solutions in place to overcome the lack of consensus. French law, under the broader notion of collaborative works, states that, in the absence of common agreement, it will be up to courts to settle the dispute.[113] German law provides that a joint author cannot refuse the publication, exploitation or alteration against good faith.[114] Italian and Portuguese laws deem the general provisions on common property applicable,[115] which means that the contribution of each author is presumed equal[116] and the disputes among the parties can be settled by the courts.[117]

The Software Directive (art.2(2)) and the Database Directive (art. 4(3)) mention "joint works" but do not define it or extract further consequences. The Term Directive (art. 1(2)), as the Berne Convention (art. 7*bis*), refers to joint authorship but leaves it likewise undefined.

2. Connected works

Connected works are works which, although independent, are combined to be exploited in common.[118] Classic examples are choreography and music

---

112 W Cornish, D Llewlyn and T Aplin, (n 32) 540 describing the situation under English law.
113 L-113-3.
114 § 8(2) UrhG. Similarly § 11(2) ÖUrhG provides that a co-author can sue the remainder for consent when the refusal has no sufficient reason (*ohne ausreichenden Grund*).
115 Art. 10 3rd paragraph ItalCA; art. 17 PTCA. See also AIPPI's summary report (n 107).
116 Art. 10 2nd paragraph ItalCA; L C Ubertazzi, 'Spunti sulla comunione in diritto d'autore' [2003] AIDA 506 (discussing whether this presumption is rebuttable); To the same effect, in English law, see *Bamgboye v Reed* [2004] 5 EMLR 61, 74. Critical of the current approach to joint authorship see L Zermer, 'Contribution and collaboration in joint authorship: too many misconceptions' [2006] JIPLP 283.
117 M Bertani, *Diritto d'autore europeo* (G. Giapichelli Editore 2011) 81.
118 Thus forming a civil law society (G Schricker and U Loewenheim, *Urheberrecht Kommentar* (4th edn C.H. Beck 2010) 263) regulated under § 705 ff. BGB (on the applicability of these rules see G Spindler, 'Miturhebergemeinschaft und BGB-Gesellschaft' in A Ohly et al (eds), *Perspektiven des Geistiges Eigentums und Wettbewerbsrecht – Festschrift für Gerhard Schricker zum 70. Geburtstag* (C.H. Beck 2005) 539).

in ballet, text and graphic arts in illustrated books or the junction of music and text in operas or songs.[119]

Some copyright statutes have specific provisions to deal with this situation. For instance the German Copyright Act provides that each author must ask for permission of the other for exploitation when according to good faith that authorization is expectable;[120] the authors remain otherwise free to exploit their work independently.[121] Though similar, the Italian regulation for composite works (*opere composte*) is very detailed and limited to music-dramatic works, musical compositions with words, choreographic works, and pantomimes.[122] The legislation tries to strike a balance by according the right to economic exploitation to the author of the most relevant work[123] and allocating the profits in the proportion of each author's contribution.[124]

3. Collective works

According to French law, collective works are those created by the initiative of one (legal or natural) person who gathers and manages the contributions of several people.[125] In this case the copyright belongs to the organizer.[126] Common examples are dictionaries,[127] encyclopaedias or newspapers.[128]

---

119 U Loewenheim, *Handbuch des Urheberrechts* (2nd edn, C.H. Beck 2010) § 11 rn1.
120 § 9UrhG.
121 Like the same lyrics with a different melody or vice-versa (U Loewenheim (n119) § 11 rn11). Art. 38 ItalCA expressly states that each of the authors of a collective work retains the right to use his own work separately. French law contains the same provision but only mentions works of different genre (L-113-3).
122 Arts. 33-37 ItalCA. T Margoni and M Perry, 'Ownership in complex authorship: a comparative study of joint works in copyright law' [2012] EIPR 22, 25-26 (describing the rules in detail and informing that some authors defend its extension by analogy).
123 V M de Sanctis, *I soggetti del dirrito d'autore* (Giuffré 2005) 88.
124 Cf art. 34 considering the author of the musical part the prevailing and art. 37, stating that where music has not the main function or value (*funzione o valore principale*) the right of exploitation belongs to the author of the pantomime, choreographic work or to the author of the literary part in the revue (*rivista musicale* – a specific kind of multi-act show).
125 L-113-2.
126 L-113-5. Same in art. 5 Dutch Copyright Act and arts. 7 and 38 ItalCA..
127 E.g. the French *Petit Robert* decision [2005] RIDA 236.
128 M Vivant and J Navarro, *Code de la propriété intellectuelle* (Lexis nexis 2013) 185.

I – The legal framework of ownership and overlaps

Italian law has the same solution and mentions these works expressly.[129] According to Alessandro Ferreti,[130] the ownership of copyright is a normative attribution of creativity in the collective work. In fact, the copyright in the collective work is independent of the possible copyright of each contributor in his specific contribution.[131] If the contributions are distinguishable and protected by copyright, in order to exploit the collective work, its creator will still need to clear the rights regarding each contribution.[132]

As with the notion of joint works, both the Software Directive (art. 2(1)) and the Database Directive (art. 4(2)) mention the term "collective works" but leave it undefined and so does art. 1(4) of the Term Directive.

4. Copyright in cinematographic works

The protection of cinematographic works under copyright poses several challenges. These difficulties depart from the qualification: how many works are there in a film and how to look at them?[133] As stated in the "Study on the conditions applicable to contracts relating to Intellectual Property in the European Union":[134] "The ownership of rights on audiovisual works (…) raises combined issues of multiple authorships and of creation under employment and/or commission".

---

129 Arts. 3, 7 and 38 ItalCA.
130 *Diritto d'Autore* (Simone 2008) 53.
131 Although under French law the notion of collective works presupposes indistinguishable contributions.
132 K Garnett, G Davies and G Harbottle, *Copinger and Skone James on Copyright* vol I (16th edn, Sweet & Maxwell 2011) 236. A collective work is often also a collection. However, the criterion to define them is different. A collective work is a work which has more than one contributor and a collection is a work which gathers different elements (protected works or not) and "by reason of the selection and arrangement of its contents, constitutes an intellectual creation", art. 2(5) BC; see also recital 13 of the Term Directive. A murky usage of the terms is often found in literature and statutes (e.g. art. 3 ItalCA employs "collective works" (*opere colletive*) for what is really a collection).
133 On the topic see P Kamina, *Film Copyright in the European Union* (CUP 2002). The multimedia works pose analogous difficulties.
134 L Guibault and B Hugenholtz, Final Report (study no ETD/2000 /B5-3001/E/69), at 27.

The BC addresses the problem briefly in art. *14bis* but the provision is of little practical significance.[135] It is nonetheless worth pointing out the limitation contained in art. 14*bis*(2)(b), according to which: "in the countries of the Union which, by legislation, include among the owners of copyright in a cinematographic work authors who have brought contributions to the making of the work, such authors, if they have undertaken to bring such contributions, may not, in the absence of any contrary or special stipulation, object to the reproduction, distribution, public performance, communication to the public by wire, broadcasting or any other communication to the public, or to the subtitling or dubbing of texts, of the work". This provision aims at strengthening the position of the film producer and to make the exploitation of a film easier.[136]

In the EU there was (and still is) a large diversity of national solutions regarding authorship in cinematographic works.[137] Abandoning more ambitious plans of complete harmonization,[138] the Term Directive in its art. 2(1) limits itself to determine that copyright vests, "by operation of the law, directly and originally in the principal director".[139] Member states remain free to designate other co-authors.[140] Regardless of ownership the Directive (art. 2(2)) determines that the duration of copyright is calculated from the death of the last of four people listed therein.

---

135 S Ricketson and J Ginsburg (n 51) 379 ff (with a detailed analysis of the negotiations).
136 T Dreier in T Dreier and B Hugenholtz (eds), *Concise European Copyright Law* (Wolters Kluwer 2006) 62.
137 For a comparison of national laws see P Kamina (n 133) 137 ff; A Manthey, *Die Filmrechtsregelungen in den wichtigsten filmproduzierenden Ländern Europas und den USA* (Nomos 1993).
138 M Walter (n 110) 546.
139 This provision is to be distinguished from art. 1(5) of the Satellite and Cable Directive. The effect of the latter was not horizontal but limited to determining the beneficiary the right of communication to the public by satellite ("even if under national law authorship in films is attributed to another person, such as the film producer", B Hugenholtz in T Dreier and B Hugenholtz (n 136) 274). Likewise, article 2(2) of the Directive 2006/115/EC of the European Parliament and of the Council of 12 December 2006 on rental right and lending right and on certain rights related to copyright in the field of intellectual property (codified version) was limited to the allocation of the rental and lending right. See also Case C-277/10 *Martin Luksan v Petrus van der Let* (CJEU 9 February 2012) para 72, hinting at the inconformity of Austrian copyright law with the directive.
140 M Walter (n 110) 546.

II – Cases of ownership problems of overlaps

A. The case of trade marks & designs

The visual appearance of a certain product can, and often is, simultaneously protected by copyright, design and trade mark rights.[141] It is thus easy to understand why this area is such fertile grounds for overlaps.[142]

In this section I will focus on the interaction between designs and trademarks, as they provide an example of two unitary regimes overlapping.[143]

The protection under both IPRs arises out of registration. The owner of the IPR is the one in whose name the IPR is registered. In the case of designs there is no prior examination[144] and regarding Community trade marks it is limited to absolute grounds for refusal.[145]

In this overlap the main criterion to deal with the conflicts is priority in time.[146]

Prior design

If someone holds earlier rights constituting a relative ground for refusal of a trade mark[147] (s)he might file an opposition.[148] It should however be noted that the earlier rights that can be invoked in an opposition are limited to

---

141 And, to different extents, the provisions of unfair competition.
142 A Ohly, Areas of Overlap Between Trade Mark Rights, Copyright and Design Rights in German Law [2007] GRUR Int 704, 707.
143 The considerations are *grosso modo* applicable to the national harmonized systems. Very critical of this cumulation he calls a pro-monopolistic solution see G Ghidini, (n 16) 55.
144 Art. 45 CDR.
145 Art. 37 CTMR. In the EU 12 national offices differ from the OHIM in this regard, also conducting *ex officio* examination of relative grounds (cf. Max Planck Institute, 'Study on the Overall Functioning of the European Trade Mark System' available at <http://ec.europa.eu/internal_market/indprop/docs/tm/20110308_allensbach-study_en.pdf> 18.).
146 F Verkade (n 19) 71.
147 Art. 8 CTMR.
148 Art. 41 CTMR.

registered trade marks, applications for registration,[149] non-registered trade marks or "another sign used in the course of trade of more than mere local significance". This applies if the rights to that sign were (1) acquired prior to the date of application for registration of the Community trade mark, or the date of priority, and (2) that sign confers on its proprietor, according to its applicable law, the right to prohibit the use of a subsequent trade mark.[150] As stated in the OHIM Manual Concerning Opposition:[151] "In order for such signs to come within the ambit of article 8(4) they must have an identifying function, that is, they must primarily serve to identify in trade a business (business identifiers) or a geographical origin (geographical indications). (...) it does not cover other types of IPRs that are not 'signs'". Therefore, a prior design does **not** constitute a relative ground for **refusal**. It is, nonetheless, a relative ground for **invalidity**.[152] The scope of the invoked right[153] must cover the trade mark, i.e., the design owner can only invalidate the trade mark if its use would infringe his design right.[154]

Pursuant to art. 53(3) CTMR, a CTM "may not be declared invalid where the proprietor of a right referred to in paragraphs 1 or 2 consents expressly to the registration of the Community trade mark before submission of the application for a declaration of invalidity or the counterclaim." In the words of David Keeling:[155] "[the owner] cannot lead the other party on a merry dance by first agreeing to the registration and then asking for it to be cancelled". However, the text is too restrictive as "express" consent is re-

---

149 Art. 8 (2) CTMR.
150 Art. 8 (4) CTMR. For a list of these signs cf Manual of Trade Mark Practice, C.4. available at <http://oami.europa.eu/ows/rw/resource/documents/CTM/legalReferences/manual/part_c_part_4_rights_under_article%208-4.pdf> accessed 12 August 2013.
151 Ibid, 6.
152 Stating that for copyright see T-435/05 *Danjaq v OHMI – Mission Productions (Dr. No)* [2009] ECR II–2097 para 41.
153 Art. 53 (2) CTMR contains a non-exhaustive list earlier rights capable of prohibiting the use of a trademark. Copyright is mentioned in subheading (c); designs are considered industrial property rights, thus covered by subheading (d).
154 The criterion is therefore the one of design law.
155 in C Gielen and V Bombhard (eds), *Concise European trade mark and design law* (Wolters Kluwer 2011) 165.

quired.[156] This apparently prevents the possibility of implied consent.[157] It is submitted that although *express consent to the registration* is required, there might be an *implied licence to use* the design in commerce. If the design owner consents to the registration of his design as trademark by a third party, it is most likely that the use is also allowed. Any other solution would be illogical and against good faith.

If no invalidity proceedings are started within 5 years the use is tolerated and there will be coexistence, unless the registration was done on bad faith.[158]

In cases where such an implied license is not accepted it is also possible to draw on the broader notions of good faith[159] to claim abuse of rights.[160] It would constitute contradictory behaviour for a licensor, despite having only assigned design rights, to enforce his copyright against the licensee; an idea akin to licensee estoppel, the doctrine developed in patent law according to which the licensee can be barred from challenging the validity of the

---

156 Ibid (Although there is not written requirement there are obvious probatory difficulties).
157 It seems that consent is not exactly synonymous with licence. Consent would be broader and less demanding, licence would mean legally granted authorization.
158 Article 54 CTMR, on acquiescence is silent regarding the rights mentioned in art. 53(2) CTMR (D Keeling (n 155) 167 considers it puzzling), but art. 110(1) CTMR deems it applicable. It must further be added that proof of knowledge is required but in our scenario that will usually be the case.
159 For a synthesis departing from answers to 30 specific cases see S Whittaker and R Zimmerman, 'Coming to terms with good faith' in S Whittaker and R Zimmerman (eds) *Good faith in European contract law* (CUP 2000) 654, 697 (after reviewing most legislation's existing notion of abuse, the Author's state that although the English legal tradition is very resistant to the notion of abuse of rights, its reliance on equity, spite "domesticated long ago" still plays a role in the correction of the "harshness of the law").
160 The preclusive effect is expressly stated v.g. in art. 334 of the Portuguese Civil Code, art. 281 of the Greek Civil Code and § 226 BGB (even though, due to the very narrow interpretation of this article, § 242 BGB, referring to duties of good faith, is the norm used for the general principle (H Köhler, *BGB Allgemeiner Teil* (35th edn, C.H. Beck 2011) 253)) or in case law (e.g. France). The principle has also been developed by the CJEU. For a brief and comparative perspective on the notion see (with further references) A Lenaerts, 'The General Principle of the Prohibition of Abuse of Rights: A Critical Position on Its Role in a Codified European Contract Law' 6 (2010) ERPL 1121. On the abuse of rights connected to the late exercise of IPRS see T Steinke, *Die Verwirkung im Immaterialgüterrecht* (V&R unipress 2006); P M Stier, *Laches und equitable estoppel im U.S.-amerikanischen und Verwirkung im deutschen Patent- und Urheberrecht* (Carl Heymanns 2004).

licensor's patent.[161] In a recent case this line of argumentation was summarily rejected by the Cancellation Division of OHIM.[162]

Prior trade mark

If there is a prior trade mark, most of the times the design will be invalid due to the lack of novelty or, at least, individual character.[163] Besides, the trade mark (or other distinctive sign) owner (25(3) CDR) can also invalidate the design on the basis of article 25(1)(e) CDR[164] within the limits of his *ius prohibendi*, i.e. the use of the trade mark in the design[165] must be an infringing one.[166] However, due to the abstract nature of design protection,[167] in matters of invalidity, the principle of specialty is of no rele-

---

161 M Jones, 'Licensee Estoppel: an overview of the position under English and European law' [2007] JIPLP 750.
162 See below n 201 and accompanying text.
163 Art. 25(1)(b) CDR. It is nonetheless possible to have a non-invalidating disclosure in the cases of "obscure sources" (art. 7 CDR). This provision has recently been interpreted very restrictively in Case ICD 8721, Invalidity Division 14 May 2013 paras 42 ff. The BGH has recently referred for preliminary ruling a set of questions that also cover the scope of article 7 (Case C-479/12, *Gautzsch Großhandel*; see H Hartwig, 'Unregistered and registered Community design rights: further guidance expected from CJEU' [2013] JIPLP 241). In this regard the General Court has recently held that the mere registration suffices to destroy novelty (Case T-666/11 *Danuta Budziewska v OHIM – Puma* (GC 7 November 2013) (only available in French and Polish) paras 24-26).
164 For an in-depth analysis of the article see M Kolasa, *The Scope and Limits of Protection for Distinctive Signs against the Community Design* (Nomos 2012).
165 The scope of this provision is therefore broader than overlaps as defined *supra* (text accompanying n12) as it can relate to different objects and even different products.
166 Case T-608/11 Beifa Group II (GC 27 June 2013) para 83; Case T-55/12 *Su-Shan Chen* (GC 25 April 2013) para 23; Case T-148/08 *Beifa Group v OHIM – Schwan-Stabilo Schwanhäußer (Instrument d'écriture)* [2010] ECR II–1681 paras 50, 94-95; also M Kolasa, (n 164) 31.
167 Art. 36(6) CDR; C-H Massa and A Strowel, 'Community Design: Cinderella revamped' [2003] EIPR 68, 71 ("...design may arguably protect one appearance regardless of the product embodying it. This goes far beyond any "speciallity of goods" principle").

II – Cases of ownership problems of overlaps

vance.[168] Thus, the question will be only similarity of signs; similarity of goods is irrelevant.

The tests differ: whilst under art. 25(1)(b) CDR the perspective is the overall impression of the design as perceived by the informed user, the approach under 25(1)(e) is one of trade mark infringement, using the perspective of the relevant consumer.[169]

There is no equivalent provision to article 53(3) CTMR which paradoxically might lead to wider solutions regarding implied licence and consent.

Additionally, if the owner of the trade mark also qualifies as the designer, (s)he has the further possibility of either claiming ownership of the registered design in national courts[170] or, on the basis of a national court ruling, invalidate the design.[171]

Summary:

The conflicts between community trade marks and community designs are dealt with by the principle of priority in time. If there is a prior design, its owner cannot oppose the registration of the trademark but can file an invalidity action, pursuant to art. 53(2) CTMR. In case there is a prior trade mark, its owner can file an invalidity claim based both on article 25(1)(b) and 25(1)

---

168 A different option would be to pay attention (for this purpose) either to the Locarno classification or to the foreseeable use of a specific design. If, in any case, attention would be given to these aspects I believe it should be in a *de minimis* fashion, only if the foreseeable use is clearly different from the prior trade mark's scope.

169 Case *Su-Shan Chen* (n 166) paras 24, 36-65 (with a thorough analysis of trade mark law infringement criteria); M Kolasa, (n 164) 70-71.G Ghidini, (n 16) 62-63 suggests that in substance the tests are the same. In Joined Cases C-101/11 P and C-102/11 P *Herbert Neuman and Others v José Manuel Baena Grupo SA* (CJEU 18 October 2012) the applicant owned a prior trade mark and accordingly relied on both grounds but ended appealing only on the basis of art. 25 (1)(b) CDR, hence the CJEU rejected 25(1)(e) on procedural grounds (paras 71-72). However, instead of considering the trade mark as a prior design and applying the respective criteria, the Court relied on the imperfect recollection test, typical of trade mark. As H Hartwig, 'the Court of Justice: "Seated Figure"' [2013] IIC 248, 253, points out this decision "unnecessarily blurs the boundaries between trade mark and design law".

170 Art. 15 CDR. The design has to be claimed in a period of three years from publication (art. 15(3)). On this rule see below **II.C**.

171 Art. 25(1)(c) CDR. Pursuant to art. 25(2) only the designer can raise this ground of invalidity.

B. The case of trade marks & copyright

(e) CDR. Pursuant to arts. 110 and 54 CTMR acquiescence might occur in case no action is taken against the trade mark for five consecutive years and the registration of the second trade mark was not done in bad faith. The text of article 53(3) CTMR seems to constrain the use of implied licences; however it is submitted that express consent is only required for registration, whereas it might be implied for use. There is no equivalent provision in the CDR, which deems it more flexible regarding implied licences.

B. The case of trade marks & copyright

Reflecting their disparate objectives the configuration of copyright and trade mark laws is significantly different.[172] In many ways trade mark protection is dynamic (the sign as understood at present),[173] whereas copyright protection is static (the work as expressed/fixated at the time of creation). Trade mark protection aims at protecting consumers against confusion in the marketplace[174] and relies on the principle of specialty,[175] so its blocking effect is limited. On the other hand copyright protection does not depend on commercial use and is not limited to a certain field of activity, whilst its infringement, in contrast with the objective protection of trade marks, requires proof of copying.[176] In the EU trade mark rights are acquired through registration[177] whereas copyright comes into existence with the act of cre-

---

172 G Dinwoodie, 'Trademark and copyright' (n 5) 517; C Mende and B Isaac, 'When copyright and trademark rights overlap' in N Wilkof and S Basheer (eds) (n 10) 137, 144; A Kur, 'Exceptions to Protection' (n 14) 597 fn8.
173 It is very much dependant on the meaning consumers attribute to a certain sign throughout time. This is reflected in notions such as acquired distinctiveness or genericism.
174 A Kur and T Dreier (n 58) 157 ff.
175 Art. 9 CTMR, with the exception for well-known trademarks. On the topic see I S Fhima, *Trade mark dilution in Europe and the United States* (OUP 2011).
176 n 40 .
177 Without prejudice to the unregistered trademark protection that is granted in some countries, like Germany (§ 4(2) of the *MarkenGesetz*) on the basis of use.

II – Cases of ownership problems of overlaps

ation[178] or fixation,[179] without any additional formalities.[180] In spite of these remarkable differences, there is a big potential for content overlap.[181] In fact, French courts have gone as far as protecting single words under copyright.[182]

Due to the respective operative events (creation or fixation vs. registration) copyright in a very specific work will always be prior in time over trade mark protection. However, the work might be based on a previous trademark, a very common situation when it comes to changing the graphic presentation of a mark (e.g. Google's Doodles), using it in advertisement (like Absolut vodka does) or rebranding. That situation does not constitute a real overlap as the prior trademark will not cover exactly the same object.[183] Nonetheless the trademark right is prior and its scope does cover certain uses of the secondly created work. Within its protective scope, the trade mark can prevent the exploitation of such work.[184]

What was said regarding the trade mark/design overlap applies *mutatis mutandis* to the overlap with copyright.[185] *If the owners are different, then the prior right will prevail.*[186] In this case, further difficulties accrue as there is no mandatory copyright registration and the copyrightability of specific

---

178 L-111-1; E Ulmer (n61) 129 (the UrhG does not expressly state it).
179 Section 3(2) and 3(3) of the CDPA; W Cornish, D Llewlyn and T Aplin, (n 32) 463. This is yet another difference between copyright and *droit d'auteur* systems (S V Lewinski (n 70) 44). See also Y Gendreau 'Le critère de fixation en droit d'auteur' 159 (1994) RIDA 111 (providing an analysis of the two systems in this regard and concluding that the requirement of fixation often leads to contradictory results). It should however be noted that even in *droit d'auteur* systems some works, like choreography require fixation in order to enjoy protection.
180 Art. 5(2) 1st sentence BC. S V Lewinski (n 70) 117-120.
181 As E Derclaye and M Leistner (n 10) 48-49 demonstrate.
182 Ibid 130.
183 Cf n 12 and accompanying text.
184 The analysis is layered; A Ohly, 'Areas of Overlap' (n 142) 706-707 "First, the mark may not have been used in the course of trade, Second, a purely or artistic or ornamental use may not be regarded as trade mark use (...). Thirdly, the constitutional guarantee of the freedom of the art (...) may provide a defence.".
185 Cf BoA decision of 6 July 2005 R869/2004-1 *Gallo Winery* (invalidating a CTM on the basis of prior copyright).
186 A Ohly, 'Areas of Overlap' (n 142) 706; J Jankowski (n18) 60-62.

B. The case of trade marks & copyright

signs (like titles,[187] characters,[188] shapes or slogans,[189] and the applied arts in general)[190] is of a dubious nature, varying according to jurisdiction.[191] Assessing if there is copyright and who is its owner will pose additional challenges to someone who wants to use a work as a trade mark.

In the leading case *Griggs v Evans*,[192] Griggs had commissioned an advertising agency to produce a new logo by combining two previously existing ones. This new logo was designed by Evans, a free-lancer,[193] who claimed ownership of the copyright in the logo. Later on Evans transferred his copyright to a competitor of Griggs, Raben.[194] In light of this assignment

---

187 See the excellent synthesis of J Klink, 'Titles in Europe' [2004] EIPR 290. Recently the General Court held (Case T-435/05 (n152)) that the title of the 007 movie "Dr no" did not indicate commercial origin but rather artistic origin of the film (para 25).Very critical of this decision see P Reeskamp, 'Dr No in trade mark country: a Dutch point of view' [2010] JIPLP 29.
188 R Graef, 'Die fiktive Figur im Urheberrecht' [2012] ZUM 108; A-V Gaide, 'Copyright, Trademarks and Trade Dress: Overlap or Conflict for Cartoon Characters?' in J Ginsburg and J Besek (eds) (n 5) 552.
189 J Davies and A Durant, 'To protect or not to protect? The eligibility of commercially-used short verbal texts for copyright and trade mark protection' [2011] IPQ 345. Allowing its protection under trade mark see e.g. Case C-353/03 *Société des produits Nestlé SA v Mars UK Ltd* [2005] ECR I-6135 ("have a break") and Case C-398/08 P Audi AG v OHIM [2010] ECR I-535 ("Vorsprung durch Technik").
190 See also below **II.C**.
191 For instance, traditionally German courts would apply more stringent requirements for copyright protection of applied arts (§ 2(1)(4) UrhG). These were distinguished from the fine arts by their intended use (*Gebrauchszweck*) and their form of production (T Dreier and G Schulze (n 13) § 2 rn158). Regarding applied arts there was a stricter requirement of originality (*see* notably BGH [1995] GRUR 581 *Silberdiestel*). Hence, it was likely that, unless they were classified as pure art, few logos or slogans would enjoy copyright protection. (E Derclaye and M Leistner (n 10) 240). Of course that, as stated in the *Silberdiestel* decision, the higher requirement of originality was accompanied by a lower threshold in the field of unfair competition: competitive individuality (*wettbewerbliche Eigenart*) which in some cases led to the same practical result in protecting against imitation). However, on 13 November 2013 the BGH (I ZR 143/12 – *Geburtstagzug*) abandoned this double standard (*Stufentheorie*). It justified that change not on the basis of EU copyright law but due to 2004 reform of German design law. Defending the double standard in the context of the design/copyright overlap *see* E Derclaye and M Leistner (n 10) 236. On the debate on originality in the EU see n 225 .
192 n 30 .
193 Ibid [11]. Thus the work for hire provision was not applicable.
194 At [12] it is said "While it might not be strictly accurate to say they are a competitor of Griggs, it is clear that they must be regarded as an enemy".

II – Cases of ownership problems of overlaps

and some litigation in Australia, Griggs started an action seeking an order that the copyright would be formally assigned to him.[195]

Applying the copyright statute the Court concluded that Griggs was indeed the owner of copyright, but immediately added:[196]

> "However, it is well established that this refers to the *legal* title to the copyright. But it is possible for a person to own the legal title to property, not for his own benefit, but for the benefit of another person. That other person is said to be the owner in *equity*. It is well established that the section 11 of the Copyright Act does not purport to legislate for equitable ownership, which is left to a well-established body of rules that have been built up by the courts over many generations. For example, suppose a free-lance designer orally agrees with a company that he shall create a website for use in its business, for payment, and on terms that the copyright shall belong to the company. Because the designer is not an employee of the company the legal title to the copyright belongs to him, because the Copyright Act says so; but the equitable title belongs to the company. This means that the designer can be called upon to assign the legal title to the copyright to the company; and, if he refuses, the law will compel him to do so"

And the Court proceeded to consider the law on implied terms of contract, stating:[197]

> "It seems to me that when a free-lance designer is commissioned to create a logo for a client, the designer will have an uphill task if he wishes to contend that he is free to assign the copyright to a competitor. This is because, in order to give business efficacy to the contract, it will rarely be enough to imply a term that the client shall enjoy a mere licence to use the logo, and nothing more. In most cases it will be obvious, it will "go without saying", that the client will need further rights. He will surely need some right to prevent others from reproducing the logo".

After analysing the specific circumstances in which the logo had been created Peter Prescott QC gave judgement for Griggs, granting him equitable ownership of the copyright[198] and confessed to be "glad to do so. The proposition that the copyright in this important logo belongs to Raben is one that

---

195 Ibid [14].
196 Ibid [33].
197 Ibid [36].
198 A second judgement ([2005] 2 WLR 513) followed on whether the determination of equitable ownership also covered foreign copyrights. The answer was in the affirmative. This approach was later followed in *Lucasfilms Ltd v Ainsworth* [2009] EWCA Civ 1328 [163].

[he] find[s] astonishing".[199] This was deemed to be a "common sense approach".[200]

This line of argumentation was recently tested and refused before the Cancellation Division of OHIM in "twin decisions" appreciating the same set of facts in relation to two trade mark registrations.[201] In 1998, Deepend Fresh Recovery, a London based design company, was commissioned to create a brand for Fresh Trading Limited's smoothie products. Mr Streek, an employer of Deepend, came up with this logo:

whose copyright, by s.11 CDPA, was owned by Deepend.[202] No written assignment to Fresh Trading had been produced. Nevertheless, in 2001 Fresh Trading registered the work as a trade mark and, in 2009, Deepend filed a request for invalidity on the grounds of 53(2)(c) CTMR.

In its defence Fresh Trading argued on the basis of equitable ownership, acquiescence and estoppel. In just two paragraphs the Cancellation division dismissed the arguments and declared the invalidity of the trade mark. The claim to equitable ownership was rejected on the basis of insufficient evi-

---

199 *Griggs v Evans* (n 30) [55].
200 C Mende and B Isaac (n 172) 148. More critic see L Bently, 'Interpretation of Copyright Rules: The Role of the Interpreter – the Creation Function' available at <http://www.cipil.law.cam.ac.uk/Judicial%20Creativity%20in%20Copyright%20Interpretation.pdf> accessed 31 August 2013 ("It is clear, then, that there are reasons to doubt the legitimacy of the judicial creativity which the *Griggs* decision represents."). A similar case *Warner v Gestetner Ltd* [1988] EIPR D89-90 was also decided – under the previous law – in favour of the commissioner to the detriment of Mr Warner, "a known commercial illustrator specializing in cats and dogs".
201 Decisions of the cancellation division of 15 November 2012, 3555C and 3556C (the paragraphs and pages are the same).
202 Ibid para 29.

dence[203] and the same reason was presented to reject estoppel.[204] It was stated: "according to article 54, acquiescence is not possible in relation to the rights covered by article 53(2) CTMR".[205] This seems wrong as art. 110 CTMR deems acquiescence applicable to earlier national rights.[206]

As the OHIM considers national law as an issue of fact[207] it is unclear how willing it will be to accept argumentations justified both on the basis of implied licence or abuse of rights when the national law is proven beyond reasonable doubt.

Summary:

In case a real overlap occurs, copyright is always prior in time due to its operative fact: protection arises out of creation or fixation. There are, nonetheless, relevant cases of prior trade mark conflicting with a later work. Priority in time is the criterion to solve the conflict. The OHIM is apparently hostile to argumentation relying on ownership in equity or estoppel.

C. The case of registered designs & copyright

The interaction of designs and copyright is one of the most controversial and explored overlaps, a truly vexed question. Nevertheless, in the field of designs, "issues of cumulation or convergence of rights are with us as never before".[208]

Article 2(7) BC states: "it shall be a matter for legislation in the countries of the Union to determine the extent of the application of their laws to works of applied art and industrial designs and models, as well as the conditions under which such works, designs and models shall be protected." The extent of this overlap is mainly determined by copyright legislation. In the EU the legislator has stated in article 17 of the Design Directive (and similarly in art. 96(2) CDR) that:

---

203 Ibid para 30.
204 Ibid para 31.
205 Ibid.
206 C Gielen in C Gielen and V Bombhard (n 155) 269.
207 Case T-579/10 *macros* (GC 7 May 2013) para 75.
208 W Cornish, D Llewlyn and T Aplin (n 32) 606-7.

"A design protected by a design right registered in or in respect of a Member State in accordance with this Directive shall also be eligible for protection under the law of copyright of that State as from the date on which the design was created or fixed in any form. The extent to which, and the conditions under which, such a protection is conferred, including the level of originality required, shall be determined by each Member State."

Up until now, the national attitudes in this regard have differed to a considerable extent. The existing approaches are usually divided in three categories:
- No cumulation, relying on a requirement of separability, according to which only the separate ornamental elements can be protected by copyright but not a piece that is simultaneously aestethic and functional. This was the old Italian approach of *scindibilità*[209] and is the current position in the US.[210]
- Partial cumulation, requiring additional "filtering requirements" such as an higher threshold of originality and/or artistic quality,[211] registration or a maximum number of reproductions,[212] for the design to be protected

---

[209] According to art. 2 number 4 of the previous law, copyright could only be granted to the works of applied art if its artistic merit could be detached from the industrial nature of the product to which it was applied. In 2001 (with *Decreto Legislativo 2 febbraio 2001, n. 95 Attuazione della direttiva 98/71/CE relativa alla protezione giuridica dei disegni e dei modelli*) the Italian legislator, transposing the Design Directive amended its copyright law, adding a new number 10 to art. 2 of its Copyright Act, according to which "the works of industrial design that are creative and have artistic value" are now protected by copyright. See P Fabio, *Disegni e Modelli* (Cedam 2011) 185-194.

[210] 17 USC § 101 (definition of 'pictorial, graphic and sculptural work').

[211] That is the case of current Italian Law. According to Vanzetti and Di Cataldo, *Manuale di Diritto Industriale* (7th edn, Giuffré 2012) 533, the requirement of artistic value – an exception to the general rule of copyright according to which merit is irrelevant – is justified by considerations of freedom of competition: the market cannot tolerate such a long right without a control of merit (*meritevolezza*). This has mainly been established by way of comparison with analogous products (V M de Sanctis, *Manuale del Nuovo Diritto d'autore* (Scientifica 2010) 60).

[212] Section 52 CDPA limits copyright of a "mass-produced" artistic work (defined as more than 50 copies, with a few exclusions) to 25 years. For a summary explanation of the current status of the law and the proposed change *see* D Amor, 'Protecting Italian Lamps and Egg Chairs: Proposed Repeal of Section 52 CDPA (UK)' 26 (2010) WIPR 30.

II – Cases of ownership problems of overlaps

under copyright.[213] This is found in Germany[214] and also in recent decisions of Portuguese[215] and Spanish[216] courts.
- Full cumulation, based on a certain understanding of the theory of the unity of the art (attributed to Eugéne Pouillet),[217] found in Belgium,[218] the Netherlands,[219] and France.[220]

In a recent (and, according to Lionel Bently, wrong)[221] decision – *Flos v Semeraro* – the CJEU held cumulation of copyright and designs, either reg-

---

213 Analysing some of the criteria *see* Y Gaubiac, 'La théorie de l'unité de l'art' 111 (1982) RIDA 3, 43 ff; G Chabaud, *Le Droit d'auteur des Artistes & des Fabricants* (Gazette du Palais 1908) 88 ff. For a broader and updated analysis cf S V Gompel and E Lavik, 'Quality, Merit, Aesthetics and Purpose: An inquiry into EU Copyright law's eschewal of other criteria than originality' 236 (2013) RIDA 100.
214 See n191. It should be made clear that, although a higher requirement of originality has been abandoned, the BGH has not opted for a full cumulation model. According to the Court in the *Geburtstagzug* decision, it is needed that the design "in view of the circles reasonably receptive to and familiar with the arts, has a level of originality that allows to speak of an artistic achievement" [rn26].
215 Process 1607/10.3TBBRG.G1, decision by Guimarães Court of Appeal of 27 February 2012 (see N Sousa e Silva, 'No copyright protection for tap designs – says Portuguese Court' [2013] JIPLP 686).
216 Decision 561/2012 (official publication number STS 6196/2012), by the Civil Section of The Spanish Supreme Court, 27 September 2012 (see N Sousa e Silva, 'Novelty is not enough: Spanish Supreme Court rejects unity of the art in an enigmatic decision' [2013] JIPLP 825).
217 *Traité théorique et pratique de propriété littéraire et artistique et du droit de représentation* (3rd edn, Paris 1908) 96. However, as Greffe and Greffe, *Traité des dessins et des modèles*, (8th edn, Lexis Nexis 2008) 51 point out, Pouillet's thesis "was far from having the absolute character that it gained afterwards".
218 E Derclaye, 'La Belgique: un pays de cocagne pour les créateurs de dessins et modèles' 14.2 (2009) Intellectuel rechten- Droits intellectuels 100, 104; C-H Massa and A Strowel, 'Le cumul du dessin ou modèle et du droit d'auteur : orbites parallèles et forces d'attraction entre deux planètes indépendantes mais jumelles' in A Cruquenaire and S Dusollier (eds) (n 11) 21, 27.
219 A K Sanders, '100 years of copyright – The Interface with design law coming full circle?' in B Hugenholtz, A Quaedvlieg and D Visser (eds) (n92) 99, 109.
220 Greffe and Greffe (n 217) 49 (their contention that France is the only country in the EU which has total cumulation is inexact).
221 'The return of industrial copyright' [2012] EIPR 654, analysing in detail the *travaux préparatoires* for the design, the Infosoc and the term directives and concluding that the field of cumulation should be left entirely to Member States and the only implication of Article 17 of the Design Directive is that "condition on the extent of protection could not be such as to prevent its existence" (at 659).

istered or unregistered, to be mandatory.[222] In paragraph 34 of the decision it is stated:

> "However, it is conceivable that copyright protection for works which may be unregistered designs could arise under other directives concerning copyright, in particular Directive 2001/29, if the conditions for that directive's application are met, a matter which falls to be determined by the national court."

The extension to which this decision imposes a European "unity of the art" and requires Member-States to adopt the full cumulation approach is still very uncertain.[223] In the past it was believed that even though the principle of cumulation had been adopted, Member-States could still decide on the conditions of protection for applied arts in their respective copyright laws.[224] As the CJEU has undertaken an ongoing interpretation of the notion of originality on the basis of Directive 2001/29, most notably in *Infopaq*, these debates remain linked and thus an area of incognita.[225]

However, neither the copyright directives, nor the design regulation (or directive) or CJEU's case-law provide much guidance on how to solve the problem at hand.

---

222 Case C-168/09 [2011] ECR I-181.
223 Following a minimalist reading see S Ricketson and U Suthersanen, 'The design/copyright overlap: is there a resolution?' in N Wilkof and S Basheer (eds), (n 10) 159,176.
224 See T Dreier in T Dreier and B Hugenholtz (n 136)16. Following Joined cases C-92/92 and C-326/92 *Phill Collins* [1993] ECR I-5145, the CJEU, in Case C-28/04 *Tod's* [2005] ECR I-5781, had made clear that the principle of non-discrimination (now art. 18 TFEU) would forestall the rule of reciprocity (art. 7 (4) BC) from operating.
225 Case C-5/08 *Infopaq International A/S v Danske Dagblades Forening* [2009] ECR I-6569 paras 36-38 (confirmed, i.a. in Case C-393/09 *Bezpečnostní softwarová assoçiasse (BSA)* [2010] ECR I-13971 paras 44-46; Joined cases C-403/08 and C-429/08 *Football Dataco* (CJEU 4 October 2011) paras 97-98). On the debate on *Infopaq* and its progeny, including its impact on Germany see (with further references) M Leistner, 'Der europäisches Werkbegriff' [2013] ZGE 4-45 (specially 30 ff). More sceptical about the effects of the decision on UK law see A Rahmatian, 'Originality in UK Copyright Law: The Old "Skill and Labour" Doctrine Under Pressure [2013] IIC 4. For a summary cf M V Eechoud, 'Along the Road to Uniformity – Diverse Readings of the Court of Justice Judgments on Copyright Work' [2012] JIPITEC 60; E Rosati, *Originality in EU Copyright – Full Harmonization through Case Law* (EE 2013).

II – Cases of ownership problems of overlaps

Under the CDR the creator of the design is designated 'designer',[226] and has the right to be mentioned in the register, regardless of ownership. [227] Pursuant to art. 14 CDR, the right to the design shall be vested in the creator (or joint creators) of the design, unless the "design is developed by an employee in the execution of his duties or following the instructions given by his employer" (art. 14(3) CDR). If someone other than the owner has registered the design, the latter will have the option to either invalidate the design[228] or to claim it as his own.[229] In this last case, third parties exploiting the design in good faith (prior to the ownership challenge) can continue their exploitation on the basis of a non-exclusive statutory licence.[230]

In *FEIA*[231] the CJEU drew on the chosen terms employer and employee,[232] to hold that article 14(3) CDR was to be interpreted restrictively and did not cover designs produced under commission.[233] The Court emphasised, nevertheless, that a design can be transferred by contractual assignment,[234] subject to the national applicable law.[235] It is not clear whether the CJEU considers implied terms of assignment admissible. It is submitted that the decision refers only to the notion of employee and Courts remain free, *per* art. 14(3) *in fine*, to consider implied licences or transfer. Furthermore, Member-States retain the possibility to establish a legal presumption of assignment.

At first sight this decision might seem to promote convergence with copyright ownership. And it is so, if we consider the *droit d'auteur* paradigm: a restrictive interpretation of article 14(3) CDR will tend to concentrate the copyright and the design right in the same person, the creator. However, it

---

226 D Stone, *European Union Design Law* (OUP 2012) 90 "…the designer is the person who designs the design".
227 Art. 18 CDR. This is a limited (the provision only refers to the register) moral right of paternity (D Musker in C Gielen and V Bombhard (n 155) 387).
228 Art. 25(1)(c) CDR.
229 Art. 15 CDR.
230 Art. 16(2) CDR.
231 Case C-32/08 *FEIA v Cul de Sac* [2009] ECR I-5611.
232 Ibid paras 45-48 and Opinion of the AG paras 27 ff. analysing the drafting history of the regulation.
233 Ibid para 49 ("… the term 'employee' refers to the person who works under the instruction of his 'employer' when developing a Community design in the context of the employment relationship.").
234 And not only the cases of inheritance or succession or merger between companies, as contended by the Commission (Opinion of the AG para 43).
235 Ibid para 81.

is also possible that by application of certain provisions of copyright law we will end up with a situation where the copyright is owned by the commissioner or organizer of a collaborative work and the design right belongs to the designer. In any case, if there is overlap, split ownership still occurs in the context of an employment situation in countries where there is no work for hire doctrine.

In these situations it could be argued that the unitary right provisions prevail (as they are EU law) and the acquisition of copyright is meaningless. This does not seem to be a sound reasoning because the hierarchical principle has no application in this context. As seen the rule is coexistence.[236] Thus, in case of split ownership of copyright and design the rule will still be priority in time. The owner of prior copyright can invalidate the design in proceedings before the OHIM on that ground.[237] Like the owner of a prior trade mark,[238] the owner of a prior design can prevent the exploitation of a work inasmuch it falls within its scope.

Most of the times the split ownership will happen after creation, resulting from the transfer of just one of the IPRs.

If a designer has granted her design rights but not the copyright she surely cannot claim the design as her own, but can she still make use of her copyright? It seems abusive and against good faith. In those cases it might be argued that the transfer in title of design rights by the designer implies at least a copyright licence or even that it is (or should be) impossible to transfer the rights separately. This last solution is found in countries following the theory of the unity of the art, either developed by jurisprudence[239] or in specific legislative provisions.[240] The implied licence solution is probably the "lowest common denominator" among the European jurisdictions for this scenario.

Another rule found e.g. in France[241] or in the Netherlands[242] is the presumption of ownership of copyright in favour of the (legal or natural) person

---

236 n 59.
237 25(1)(f) CDR. A recent example of an application relying on both prior copyright and lack of individual character (without success) is Case T-68/11 *Erich Kastenholz v OHIM* (GC 6 June 2013).
238 See text accompanying n 184 .
239 E Derclaye and M Leistner (n 10) 121.
240 A K Sanders (n 219) 110-111.
241 Greffe and Greffe (n 217) 293 ff.
242 Art. 8 Dutch Copyright Act. Similarly see art.14(3) PTCA.

II – Cases of ownership problems of overlaps

that exploits the work.[243] This is a practical and important way to overcome the burdensome proof of ownership in infringement actions. The rule can have the equivalent effect to granting ownership,[244] at least against third parties. It is nonetheless a rebuttable presumption and will not be of great use in situations of conflict between the different IPRs' owners.

Summary:

Concerning the cumulation of design and copyright there are still very different solutions among Member-States, although the CJEU might be developing a "european unity of the art" on the basis of its interpretation of EU copyright. Art 14 CDR establishes a work for hire doctrine regarding the design right which, according to the CJEU, is to be interpreted restrictively. That will tend to concentrate initial ownership. Thus split ownership will mainly be the result of contractual arrangements. The criterion for conflicts is still priority in time. However, at least in the case of contractual arrangements referring to just one of the cumulated right there might be an implied licence regarding the other.

D. The case of databases: sui generis right & copyright

In 1996, a Directive on the legal protection of databases was adopted. According to that Directive, a database can be protected by two rights: copyright, if the database constitutes the author's own intellectual creation[245] and a *sui generis* right, if substantial investment was put into its creation.[246] Though the object of protection differs – copyright focuses on the original selection or arrangement whereas the *sui generis* right protects the invest-

---

243 This is to be distinguished from the presumption of authorship found in art. 15 BC stemming from the display of a name in the work. In this case the significant event is the exploitation and not the display of a name.
244 J Seignette 'Authorship' (n 92) 135("…creating a *de facto* allocation rule for copyright in commissioned works…").
245 Art. 3 DatD.
246 Art. 7 DatD.

D. The case of databases: sui generis right & copyright

ment in the gathering of data[247] and its presentation[248] – the potential for overlaps is almost unlimited.[249]

Pursuant to article 4, copyright will be vested in the creator of that database, a natural person unless the national law of the Member State allows for legal persons to acquire copyright.[250] The rule has no "hard" content, it only suggests a solution but Member-States retain their freedom to regulate the matter.[251] If the work has been created by a group of people then these will be joint owners.[252] In case the national legislation has specific provisions to deal with collective works, the economic rights shall be owned by the person holding the copyright.[253] Unlike the Computer Programs Directive's art. 2(3) and the Initial Proposal's art. 3(4), there is no provision dealing with databases created by employees.[254] The harmonizing effect of these rules is therefore minimal.[255]

According to article 7 and Recital 41, the maker of the database, the person (quite often a company) who takes the initiative and the risk of investing is the owner of the *sui generis* right.[256]

---

247 But not in the creation of data as results from the CJEU decision in Case C-203/02 *BHB v William Hill* [2004] ECR I-10415 paras 30-42. M Davidson and B Hugenholtz, 'Football fixtures, horse races and spin-offs: the ECJ domesticates the database right' [2005] EIPR 113.

248 M Leistner, 'The protection of databases' in E Derclaye, *Research handbook* (n 51) 427, 431.

249 Art. 7(4) DatD. A Quaedvlieg, 'Overlap/relationships' (n 63) 483 stating "these rights were meant to cumulate". That seems, however, to be an overstatement as the Initial Proposal (Proposal for a Council Directive on the legal protection of databases. COM (92) 24 final, 13 May 1992), in its art. 2 (5), provided that the *sui generis* right would not apply where the database was already protected by copyright or neighbouring rights.

250 Art. 4(1) DatD.

251 Recital 29 DatD. B Hugenholtz in T Dreier and B Hugenholtz (eds) (n 136) 319. See also M Leistner, D*er Rechtsschutz von Datenbaken im deutschen und europäischen Recht* (C.H. Beck 2000) 84 ff.

252 Art. 4(3) DatD. B Hugenholtz ibid 320 ("The wording of art. 4(1) suggest that a group of natural persons may also qualify as the author, but as para. 3 clarifies, what is meant here is joint authorship.").

253 Art. 4(2) DatD.

254 B Hugenholtz in T Dreier and B Hugenholtz (eds) (n 136) 320.

255 Nevertheless it had some effects. V.g. Belgium has a "work for hire" provision for databases (art. 20*ter* of the Belgian copyright act). Similar provision is art. *12bis* ItalCA (creating a presumption of transfer for databases).

256 Laddie, Prescott and Vitoria (n 97) 1287 ("It should be noted that this need not be the person who actually does the work. Indeed it often will not be.").

II – Cases of ownership problems of overlaps

Although this framework regarding the ownership of both rights is fertile ground for different ownerships of different rights in the same database, it seems that the legislator has not predicted the problem.[257] Thus situation poses difficulties not only for the owners of the rights who want to exploit it but also for users, who might only have obtained a licence from one of the two relevant rightholders.[258]

Even though that was not the main object of the dispute (nor the preliminary ruling), in *Directmedia*[259] there was a copyright owner in an anthology of German poetry, Mr. Knoop, working for the University in Freiburg, and the database right, owned by the University, who had spent €34.900 throughout the two and half years it took to compile the database.[260] A third party (Directmedia) was sued on the basis of infringement of both copyright and the *sui generis* right. As the applicable law to determine copyright ownership was German law, the owners were different.

In this case, there is no prevalence in time as both IPRs are born simultaneously in the sphere of the two subjects.[261] There seems to be no hierarchy or precedence either. According to the law as it is, the investor and the copyright owner would need to get permission from each other in case they want to exploit the database.[262] Most of the times this will mean that the owner of the *sui generis* right will need to bargain a license anew.

Normally, the copyright owner is either an employee or a commissioned person; thus it can be argued that the original creation has already been remunerated. Such payment was part of the substantial investment; hence (at

---

257 A Quaedvlieg, 'Overlap/relationships' (n 63) 516.
258 Laddie, Prescott and Vitoria (n 97) 1287 ("Users of a database must take great care to consider (...) whether a licence would be required from both owners").
259 C-304/07 *Directmedia Publishing GmbH v Albert-Ludwigs-Universität Freiburg* [2008] ECR I-7565.
260 Ibid paras 9-15.
261 F Macrez (n 11) 103 (stating without elaborating on the consequences : "in case of conflict, the balance should tilt in favour of copyright"). There seems to be no justification for such solution. Lucas and Lucas (n 71) 953 state twice that "It is enough to apply in a distributive fashion the rules which do not have the same scope of application". This enigmatic sentence can be seen as a timid suggestion of prevalence.
262 "This may enable either party to prevent the other from making commercial use of the database, unless either or both can rely on lawful user rights to disable the other's controls or on some other legal principle" (S Chalton, 'The Copyright and Rights in Databases Regulations 1997: some outstanding issues on implementation of the Database Directive' [1998] EIPR 178, 181).

D. The case of databases: sui generis right & copyright

least) a license is implied.[263] This argumentation will face some obstacles, such as formalities,[264] burden of proof, specific legal provision on the contrary[265] and a general attitude *favor auctoris*,[266] regarding the author as the weakest party[267] and ownership rules as imperative.[268]

In the judgement *Ray v Classic FM*,[269] Mr. Robin Ray, "nationally famous for his encyclopaedic knowledge of classical music",[270] had concluded a consultancy agreement with Classic fm to advise on the programming and repertoire of the broadcaster. This agreement was silent on the subject of

---

263 Making that argument *see* A Bertrand, *Droit d'auteur* (3rd edn, Dalloz 2010) 185. Against it *see* Lucas and Lucas (n 71) 180 ff. This has been followed in some decisions (Y Gaubiac (n 213) 14 ff). In Germany the BGH in *Wetterführungspläne* [2001] GRUR 155, seems to have followed that logic by holding that "when a computer program is developed in the framework of a worker's duties he shall not be entitled to additional remuneration if that is patented". As seen, under UK law, the extent of this problem seems to be minimal. Either by operation of the work for hire doctrine or due to implied terms, including equitable ownership of copyright or an implied licence, the database maker will not have problems. A similar effect can be achieved in Germany through an implied licence (see below **III.B.3**).

264 See L Guibault and B Hugenholtz (n134) 31-32 and a country-by-country survey at 37 ff..

265 See n 100.

266 K Aarab, 'Droit d'auteur et droit des dessins et modèles : le conflit de la recevabilité à agir des personnes morales' 68 (2011) Revue Lamy Droit de l'immatériel 97; T Dreier and G Schulze (n 13) § 31 rn 110 ("The copyright tends to remain with the author as much as possible"). Even though "contrary to the law of a number of Member States German copyright law does not follow the rule *"in dubio pro auctore"*" (L Guibault and B Hugenholtz (n 134) 82).

267 P Katzenberger, 'Protection of the Author as the Weaker Party to a Contract under International Copyright Contract Law' [1988] IIC 731.

268 A Dietz, 'Das Urhebervertragsrecht in seiner rechtspolitischen Bedeutung' in F-K Beier et al. (eds) *Urhebervertragsrecht* (C.H. Beck 1995) 1. A counter-argument is that the same effect (protecting the author's interest) can be achieved (maybe in an even more efficient way) by guaranteeing the author equitable remuneration and the maintenance of his moral rights (cf. 165(3) PTCA). This represents a certain convergence with the employee's invention logic. Pointing out, in the wider context of imperative contractual laws protecting authors, that often these authors do not "dare to insist on the application of such provisions" *see* S V Lewinski, 'Collectivism and its role in the frame of individual contracts' in in J Rosén (ed) (n) 117,118 stating the same for the model adopted by German Law (at 120).

269 [1998] ECC 488.

270 Ibid [4].

Intellectual Property.[271] Ray developed a star system to rate the items in the playlist which was to be managed by means of a computer program (Selector) aimed at optimizing the selection of music played.[272] Throughout the duration of his contract Mr. Ray individually classified 50,000 items of music according to his star system.[273] The system worked so well that Classic fm wanted to licence the database.[274] Mr. Ray considered that constituted infringement of his copyright – not on the database but on documents contained in it – and sued Classic fm. After having dismissed the Defendant's claim to ownership under s.11(2) the Court proceeded to analyse the issue of ownership in equity beginning with a thorough review of the law. In face of the facts Justice Ligthman found implied a licence "for the purpose of enabling the Defendant to carry on its business"[275] and thus upheld the claim for infringement. The issue of estoppel was dismissed as unfounded.[276]

Summary:

The *sui generis* right protecting investment and copyright can and very often will cumulate in a certain database. When that happens, although some authors suggest prevalence of the copyright owner, it seems that there is a blocking situation as there is no priority in time (both rights arise simultaneously). In case the copyright owner is commissioned or an employee there might be an implied licence. However such an argumentation will face obstacles due to laws driven by the protection of the author.

---

271 Ibid [6].
272 Ibid [8]. Although databases are distinct from software – software is code, "any set of machine-readable instructions (most often in the form of a computer program) that directs a computer's processor to perform specific operations."(<https://en.wikipedia.org/wiki/Software> accessed 23 August 2013), whilst a database is an organized collection of data (<https://en.wikipedia.org/wiki/Database> accessed 23 August 2013) – they are usually part of the same product and, as this case shows, often the value of a computer program is due to the "database on which the code operates" (T J McIntyre, 'Copyright in custom code: Who owns commissioned software?' [2007] JIPLP 473, 484). This is not a real overlap, as the object is different, but can pose similar difficulties. On the technical and legal notions see M Leistner, *Der Rechtsschutz* (n 251) 41 ff.
273 Ibid [10].
274 Ibid [11].
275 Ibid [48].
276 Ibid [51].

E. The case of software and computer implemented inventions

The protection of software was and still is a very controversial issue.[277] After much debate, at the European level, it was decided to bring it under copyright[278] by means of a Directive,[279] the first on copyright matters. This solution was later incorporated in the TRIPS Agreements, art. 10 (1), which states: *computer programs whether in source or object code, shall be protected as literary works under the Berne Convention.*

At the same time Patent Offices around the world issue the so-called software patents or, in EPO's terminology, "computer implemented inventions".[280] To be accurate, one has to distinguish between the objects of protection: software, i.e. only source and object code, protected under the copyright for software,[281] and computer implemented inventions, which differ from software.[282] These patents do not directly protect software or the al-

---

277 Providing background and further references *see* R Hilty and C Geiger, 'Towards a New Instrument of Protection for Software in the EU? Learning the Lessons from the Harmonization Failure of Software Patentability' in E Arezzo and G Ghidini (eds), *Biotechnology And Software Patent Law* (EE 2011) 153.
278 As pointed out by T Dreier, 'The Council Directive of 14 May 1991 on the Legal Protection of Computer Programs' [1991] EIPR 319, 320 any neighbouring rights' or *sui generis* approach would have necessitated the creation of a new instrument for international protection. This would be a long and cumbersome process without any guarantees of success.
279 Council Directive 91/250/EEC of 14 May 1991 on the legal protection of computer programs, replaced without any substantial modification by Directive 2009/24/EC of the European Parliament and of the Council of 23 April 2009 on the legal protection of computer programs (Codified version), hereinafter **CPD**.
280 This was also the terminology employed in the failed Proposal for a Directive of the European Parliament and of the Council on the patentability of computer-implemented inventions COM/2002/0092 final [2002] OJ C 151E.
281 *Case* C-393/09 *Bezpečnostní softwarová asociace* (BSA) [2010] ECR I-13971 para 34.
282 According to the Guidelines for Examination in the European Patent Office (20 June 2012) Part G Chapter II-3.6 "Programs for computers are a form of "computer-implemented invention", an expression intended to cover claims which involve computers, computer networks or other programmable apparatus whereby prima facie one or more of the features of the claimed invention are realised by means of a program or programs".

II – Cases of ownership problems of overlaps

gorithms (computer programs *as such*),[283] they aim at the technical function(s) performed by the program.[284] The object of protections is clearly different. As stated by the CJEU in *SAS Institute*:[285] "neither the functionality of a computer program nor the programming language and the format of data files used in a computer program in order to exploit certain of its functions constitute a form of expression of that program and, as such, are not protected by copyright in computer programs".

There is no coincidence in the criteria for infringement, and there are no rules dealing with the conflict neither in copyright nor in patent laws.

If the scope of the patented computer implemented invention covers the one present in the software but was achieved by independent conception, there was no copyright infringement, for this requires copying.[286]

Even when copyright predates patent protection,[287] its protection is not dependent on an act of publicity. Therefore the patent requirement of novelty[288] is not necessarily affected. If a person who has independently reached the same technical solution succeeds in obtaining a patent for a computer implemented invention which also covers the solution found in the pre-written software there is not much left for the copyright owner.[289] Depending on

---

283 Art. 52(3) EPC. Providing some guidance on the concepts of "computer program as such" and "further technical effect" cf Opinion of the Enlarged Board of Appeal of 12 May 2010 (G3/08) (finding the referral not admissible but expending relevant considerations on the topic).

284 On the requirements and particularities of Computer Implemented Inventions *see* C Schwarz and S Kruspig, *Computerimplementierte Erfindungen – Patentschutz von Software?* (Carl Heymanns 2011).

285 Case C-406/10 *SAS Institute Inc. v World Programming Ltd* (CJEU 2 May 2012) para 46.

286 Even an independent invention might have involved copyright infringement in a certain intermediate step of its conception, like in certain cases of reverse engineering that fall out of the restrictive conditions of art. 6 CPD. In this situation the copyright protected code was just a starting point for the inventor, the performance of the invention, i.e. the exploitation of the patent, involves no copyright infringement, so there is no dependency.

287 That will always be the situation in case of a real overlap (n 12).

288 Art. 54 EPC contains what is called "an absolute requirement of novelty", any enabling disclosure to the public is enough to deny patentability (A Kur and T Dreier (n 58) 111).

289 F Macrez (n 11) 101 ("…the legal protection through copyright will not have any utility. If not in principle at least in fact, copyright is hierarchically inferior to a patent.").

E. The case of software and computer implemented inventions

the jurisdiction, (s)he might benefit from prior user rights.[290] This constitutes nothing but a defence, a limitation to the effects of the patent: the patent owner can forbid everyone but the prior user from using his invention.

A different situation arises when a computer implemented invention can be induced from certain copyright protected software and this involves no further inventive activity. In that case the patented solution is not autonomous.[291] The creative process is simultaneously inventive activity. The creator, owner of the prior copyright, is also the inventor, entitled to a patent himself.

When the person applying for the patent[292] is not entitled to it, its legitimate owner can claim it in national courts.[293] Determining who is an inventor constitutes a reasoning akin to determining who is/are the author(s).[294] The rules according to which the patent owner is determined have not been harmonized but they converge to a significant extent.[295]

Pursuant to art. 2(3) CPD: "Where a computer program is created by an employee in the execution of his duties or following the instructions given by his employer, the employer exclusively shall be entitled to exercise all economic rights in the program so created, unless otherwise provided by contract".

---

290   See n 43.
291   This is not synonymous with dependency as in "dependent patents". As copyright only protects a certain expression (art. 9(2) TRIPS) it will be relatively easy to practice the invention (defined by its function) with a different code. Even if a very similar code is written independently there will be no infringement. Hence, due to the broader scope of patent protection and the subjective requirement for copyright infringement the situation of patents dependent on copyright mentioned by C Le Stanc, 'Interférences entre droit d'auteur et droit de brevet quant a la protection du logiciel: approche française' in S K Verma and R Mittal (eds), *IPRs A global vision* 162, 167 seems unlikely to happen.
292   Any person(s) can apply for a patent (arts. 58, 59 EPC) and the applicant is presumed to be entitled to it (art. 60(3) EPC). It is necessary to distinguish those who can apply from those who are entitled to the patent.
293   Art. 61 EPC and rules 13-15 of the implementing regulation.
294   On the topic *see* R Miller et al, *Terrel on the Law of Patents* (17th edn, Sweet & Maxwell 2010) 95-99. This is particularly clear in the context of co-inventorship ("A co-inventor within the meaning of art. 60(2) [EPC] is a person who, on its own initiative, intellectually contributed a creative part to the overall inventive concept" (Hess (n 66), mentioning German jurisprudence)).
295   See n67 and accompanying text.

II – Cases of ownership problems of overlaps

This provision only requires a presumption of an exclusive licence regarding economic rights.[296] Although a broader solution covering commissioned works was to be found in the Initial proposal, it was eschewed to the benefit of freelance programmers.[297] Nonetheless some countries, like Germany,[298] when transposing the Directive extended the application of this solution to commissioned works.[299] Curiously, the UK did not, [300] but the implied terms solution has been used.[301]

Summary:

Although copyright and patents often overlap in computer programs, split ownership of those rights will not generate particular problems. In case copyright predates patent protection, a patent can still be obtained if there was no enabling disclosure and the other requirements of patentability are met. If the patentee copied the invention from the creation, he cannot be deemed the inventor and, simultaneously is infringing copyright. If the patentee has achieved the same technical solution independently (most probably with a different code) he has not infringed copyright and will be able to patent his invention. The prior copyright owner can have prior rights inasmuch the applicable law allows them.

---

296 In order to respect different traditions, specifically the monistic approach (A Metzger (n 90) 82).
297 T Dreier, 'The Council Directive' (n 278) 321.
298 § 69b(2)UrhG.
299 This seems to be admissible as the Directive "confines itself to laying down a few basic principles" (M Walter (n 110) 112). See also F Bayreuther, 'Zum Verhältnis zwischen Arbeits-, Urheber- und Arbeitnehmererfindugsrecht Unter besonderer Berücksichtigung der Sondervergütungsansprüche des angestellten Softwareerstellers' [2003] GRUR 570 (considering the issue of equitable remuneration under § 32 UrhG and the applicability of § 20 *Arbeitnehmererfindungsgesetz*). Cf n263 .
300 T J McIntyre (n272) 473.
301 V.g. *Clearsprings Management Ltd -v- Businesslink Ltd* [2005] EWHC 1487 (restricting these to a licence).

III – Possible solutions to the problem

A. The extent of the problem

The previous analysis clearly shows that the extent of the problem is smaller than what might initially seem. Not all cases of different ownerships in overlaps generate an unjustified blocking effect or remain unregulated.

As seen, if the specific overlap regards cumulation with copyright, if there is an independent creation, there is no infringement. In cases of registered IPRs priority in time is the criterion: if there is a right prior in time the registration is invalid. As copyright arises out of creation or fixation and trade mark or designs out of registration, copyright will trump registration. The requirements of novelty and individual character in design law lead to a similar result.[302]

The blocking effect arising out of split ownerships depends on the extent a certain activity constitutes infringement. One will have to determine if the exploitation of the object falls within the scope of the IPR. This operation involves not only the infringement analysis but also an assessment of the interactions with freedom of expression and artistic creation, which might constitute important exceptions to infringement.[303]

Another clear principle is: one cannot legitimately register an achievement of someone else.[304] In those cases, usually the real owner will be able to claim the respective IPRs as its own in national courts or revoke it.

These rules are logically conceived but need to be tempered with other considerations, otherwise they will fail to solve the blocking effect arising out of split ownerships, leading not only to unfair results but to granting rights without any real utility, frustrating the very justification for such concessions.

Implied licences and good faith/estoppel are two recurring approaches to our problems in the previously analysed cases. Those, among other possible solutions, will be considered below.

---

302 See n 163.
303 A Ohly, 'Areas of Overlap' (n 184).
304 Nonetheless, registers do not require prove of authorisation or licensing (n 292).

III – Possible solutions to the problem

B. A general solution?

As seen, in the EU overlap is the norm. One notable example of limiting copyright's action in light of other interests[305] is found in the CJEU decision *Dior v Evora*.[306] The Court held in a laconic statement[307] that a trade mark holder who also owned copyright in the bottles and packaging of his goods (Dior) could not enforce its copyright against a retailer where trade mark exhaustion had already operated. The reasoning, albeit inspiring,[308] has no direct utility to our problem, since exhaustion can only operate in regard to the same "origin" ("the proprietor or with his consent")[309] and our scenario is characterised by different ownership. Thus, unless some other solution operates, the actions by a certain IP right owner will violate the right of the other.

1. Avoiding the problem

a) Avoiding overlaps?

One obvious solution to the problems created would be to avoid overlaps. Even though there are "channelling" provisions,[310] rules that reduce the extent of the overlap such as a demanding copyright standard of originali-

---

305 A Quaedvlieg 'Concurrence' (n 9) 28-29, presents the case as an example of negative convergence, a limitation of both right due to the "overriding interest of the free movement of goods within the internal market and the purpose of the exhaustion rule".
306 C-337/95 *Parfums Christian Dior SA* [1997] ECR I-06013.
307 Ibid para 58 "...there being no need to consider the question whether copyright and trade mark rights may be relied on simultaneously in respect of the same product – it is sufficient to hold that (...) the protection conferred by copyright as regards the reproduction of protected works in a reseller's advertising may not, in any event, be broader than what is conferred on a trade mark owner in the same circumstances".
308 Proposing legislative changes to copyright in the aftermath of the case see A Kur, 'The "Presentation Right" – Time to Create a New Limitation in Copyright Law?' [2000] IIC 308.
309 Art. 13 CTMR.
310 Using that terminology and making an US-based analysis see V R Moffat, 'Mutant Copyrights and Backdoor Patents: the Problem of Overlapping Intellectual Property Protection' (2004) 19 Berkeley Technology Law Journal 1473.

B. A general solution?

ty[311] or the exclusions of subject matter, like the general idea of functionality in designs and trademarks.[312] But as Annette Kur points out overlaps in themselves are not a problem, it is their potential to frustrate the balances of each specific IP Right that poses new challenges and requires a horizontal approach.[313] It is nonetheless an important reflection to make, whether the amount and extent of overlaps found in the present legal framework is justified and should be maintained,[314] as in some cases the solution can lie in preventing the overlap.[315]

---

311 As already stated it remains to be seen how much independence Member States retain in the aftermath of *Infopaq*.
312 For an overview regarding trade marks and copyrights see G Dinwoodie, 'Trademark and copyright' (n 5) 506-517 and A Quaedvlieg, 'Protection of Three-Dimensional Models as a Trademark' in J Ginsburg and J Besek (eds) (n 5) 576. On the topic of functionality *see* v.g. J Cornwell, 'Dyson and Samsung Compared: Functionality and Aesthetics in the Design Infringement Analysis' [2013] EIPR 273; J Du Mont and M Janis,' Functionality in Design Protection Systems' (2012) 19 Journal of Intellectual Property Law 261.
313 'Too Pretty to Protect? Trade Mark Law and the Enigma of Aesthetic Functionality' in J Drexl, R Hilty, L Boy and C Godt (eds) (n 16) 139, 149 ("…separating between the different regimes is not an aim in itself, in the sense that the system of intellectual property law must be kept in an 'orderly' state. Instead, [the exclusion] draws its justification from the balance that must be achieved between the protection of creations, innovations and the informational value of distinctive signs, on the one hand, and free competition on the other."). See also J-C Galloux (n) 89 (overlaps are an unavoidable consequence of the diversity of IPRs); G Dinwoodie 'Trademark and copyright' (n 5) 521 "such grand plans for a unified system of intellectual property are (like a general rule governing cumulation) too grand, and perhaps too fundamental, a response to the problem".
314 A Quaedvlieg, 'Concurrence' (n 9) 26 ("Concurrent protection might in fact prove to be a sophisticated legal answer to the insatiable and multiform needs of an information and marketing economy"). In the same vein see also T Cook, 'How IPrs, like Nature, Abhor a Vacuum, and What Can Happen When They Fill it – Lacunae and Overlaps in Intellectual Property' (2012) 17 JIPR 296.
315 As mentioned above (n 249) the database maker right was to have a subsidiary nature, which would have avoided the problem of ownership altogether. G Dinwoodie 'Trademark and copyright' (n 5) 519 ("We should (…) be hesitant to impose an overarching "cumulation principle""); A Kur 'Exceptions' (n 14) 597 fn9 mentions critically the Danish solution according to which there could be no copyright in an object created with the intention to be used as a trademark.

b) Avoiding differences in ownership?

Another way of looking at the issue is from the ownership perspective. Developing parallel rules of ownership in the cases of overlaps would also solve the problem. There are different rules regarding copyright ownership throughout the EU and these remain deeply entrenched in national traditions. It seems unnecessary (and probably unfeasible) to undertake such a deep harmonization effort.[316] A less drastic solution like the one found in the computer program directive has the potential to achieve the same goals. Furthermore, even in countries, like the UK, with work-for-hire provisions, the problems are still occurring. The equitable ownership of copyright is a solution very specific to common law[317] and in clear contradiction both with the formal requirements – and, in monistic systems, the possibility – of assignment. An interesting solution found in the Wittem's group proposal for a European Copyright Code[318] consists in a work for hire provision (limited to economic rights)[319] combined with an implied licence approach to commissioned works.[320]

2. Prevalence

To solve some problems posed by overlaps some commentators submit the prevalence of the regime with the most significant relation with the case.[321] Finding which regime that is – in a private-international law like reasoning – requires systematic and teleological considerations, considering

---

316 Lucas and Lucas (n 71) seem to suggest that harmonization might follow from the notion of originality adopted in *Infopaq*. Rejecting Kreutzer's proposal of introducing exceptions to the creator's principle see M Leistner, 'Book Review – Till Kreutzer, Das Modell des deutschen Urheberrechts und Regelungslaternativen' [2011] JIPITEC 165, 167.
317 A Rahmatian (n 84) 300. Additionally, "... an equitable owner of copyright work cannot enforce its rights against a third party who buys the legal copyright in good faith without notice of the equitable owner's rights."(T Golder and A Mayer (n 20) 168).
318 Available at < http://www.copyrightcode.eu/> accessed 31 August 2013.
319 Art. 2.5.
320 Art. 2.6.
321 A Quaedvlieg 'Overlap/Relationship' (n 63) 490. This was the solution found by the Supreme Court of Russia for infringement in a design and copyright cumulation scenario (for an analysis see Annex I).

B. A general solution?

the essential function of each IPR. Even if such approach is adopted, it does not solve all cases as two or more rights might be on equal proximity to the case. Antoon Quaedvlieg calls this "cases of perfect concurrence" and though he finds them rare he also admits "in those cases only hierarchy can solve the problem".[322]

If this might be an efficient solution when dealing with questions of infringement and exceptions (the use of several rights by the same owner in a combined way to strengthen her position); in our case, allowing the prevalence of one right would mean the total irrelevance of the other. It would be meaningless to hold copyright if the design right belonging to someone else would prevail.[323] It is conceivable that this prevalence would only turn one right from property into liability,[324] the owner of the "losing" right would only be entitled to remuneration but would not be able to exclude the owner of the "winning" right. This is in line with the solution found in Italy for connected works.[325] Unless the hierarchy, or at least some criteria for the qualification are expressly stated (or developed by jurisprudence) the outcome is excessive legal uncertainty.[326]

3. Contractual or quasi-contractual solutions

a) Implied licence

In the context of a contract, it is possible to extract consequences even though they are not expressly mentioned. Under English law, these are called implied terms, which can be implied by law, in fact and on the basis of custom or trade usage.[327] For terms to be implied, as summarized by the Privy

---

322 Ibid.
323 F Verkade (n 19) 71.
324 On the distinction see the classic article by G Calabresi and A Melamed, 'Property rules, liability rules, and inalienability: one view of the cathedral' [1982] HLR 1089.
325 See supra n 122 .
326 A Quaedvlieg 'Overlap/Relationship' (n 63) 492 ("Establishing the most significant relationship is a legal technique, not a bundle of ready-made answers"). F Verkade (n 19) 73 ("…this is what lawyers are brought up on, and it's good for employment in the legal profession.").
327 N Andrews, *Contract Law* (CUP 2011) 353 ff. Also S Whittaker and R Zimmerman, 'Good faith in European contract law: surveying the legal landscape' in S Whittaker and R Zimmerman (eds) (n 159) 46.

III – Possible solutions to the problem

Council in *BP refinery (Westernport) Pty LTd v Shire of Hastings*,[328] they must: "(a) be reasonable and equitable; (b) be necessary to give business efficacy to the contract, so that no term will be implied if the contract is effective without it; (c) be so obvious that 'it goes without saying'; (d) be capable of clear expression; (e) not contradict any express term of the contract.".[329]

This is somehow a functional equivalent to a general criterion of commercial good faith.[330] In the IP field the implied terms can be either an assignment or a licence. Due to the reluctance of most author's rights systems to deprive authors from their copyright and the usual formal requirements for assignment, the notion that is more apt to be considered is the one of implied licence.

In certain situations even though no express authorization is granted, it results from the circumstances that specific acts, which would otherwise be infringement, were authorized. For instance, if a reader writes to a newspaper, it can be presumed that the publication is authorized.[331] Along the same lines, if an investor pays the employee to create a database or the company commissions a designer to produce a logo, it can be said that a licence results from the circumstances.[332] Under German Law, according to the "purpose of transfer" doctrine (*Zweckübertragunsgslehre*)[333] a licence might be implied if it results from the objectives of a certain contract. This rule has a big practical significance and often leads to results equivalent to the work for hire doctrine.[334]

The thesis of implied licences in the context of employment, limited to the needs of the employer is contentious. In France, despite having some

---

328 180 CLR 266 (1977).
329 For the discussion on the officious bystander and business efficacy tests and the doctrine in general *see* R Austen-Baker, *Implied Terms in English Contract Law* (EE 2011).
330 N Andrews (n 327) 375. See also n 159 .
331 W Cornish, D Llewlyn and T Aplin (n 32) 536-537.
332 In that sense see the decision of the Munich Regional Court of 13 June 2007 ZUM-RD [2007] 498, 502.
333 Pursuant to § 31(5) UrhG when a contract does not expressly mention the forms of exploitation covered these are to be determined according to the purpose of the contract.
334 T Dreier and G Schulze (n 13) § 43 rn1. In a certain sense the German solution is even wider as it also covers commissioned works; A Metzger (n90) 83; H-P Götting, 'Urheberrechtliche und vertagsrechtliche Grundlagen' in F-K Beier et al. (eds) (n 268) 53, 72.

defenders[335] this thesis is denied by the majority[336] for it would, as Strowel points out, deprive L 111-3 of meaning.[337] In Germany an implied licence is normally accepted inasmuch the creation results from the nature of the contract.[338]

In the different context of exhaustion the CJEU has dealt with the concept of implied licence. The issue in *Davidoff*[339] was whether the consent of the trade mark holder could be implied or had to be explicit. The Court held that the licence "may be implied, where it is to be inferred from facts and circumstances prior to, simultaneous with or subsequent to the placing of the goods on the market",[340] however it could not be inferred just from the absence of action by the owner.[341] According to Taina Pihlajarinne,[342] implied licence "has been seen more like an act similar to assignment and declaration of intent, on the basis of which the other party can act in good faith".

b) Abuse of rights

As Lenaerts writes: "the concept of abuse of rights refers to situations in which a right is formally exercised in conformity with the conditions laid down in the rule granting the right, but where the legal outcome is against

---

335 See supra n 263. For a comparative overview see A Lucas-Schloetter, *Les droits d'auteur des salariés en Europe continentale* (Cahiers IRPI 2004).
336 Lucas and Lucas (n 71) citing a decision of the French *Cour de cassation*. See also L Drai, *Le Droit du Travail Intellectuel* (LGDJ 2005).
337 (n 70) 326. The same position is found in Portugal (M V Rocha, 'A titularidade das criações intelectuais no âmbito da relação de trabalho' in *Nos 20 anos do Código das Sociedades Comerciais* (Coimbra Ed 2007) 167).
338 § 43 UrhG. For a recent decision regarding the work of an architect working for the State see BGH [2011] GRUR 59. See also BGH [1991] GRUR 523 *Grabungsmaterialien*; T Fuchs, 'Der Arbeitnehmerurheber im System des § 43 UrhG' [2006] GRUR 561; R Kraßer, 'Urheberrecht in Arbeits-, Dienst- und Auftragsverhältnissen' in F-K Beier et al. (eds) (n 268) 77.
339 Joined Cases C-414/99 to C-416/99 *Zino Davidoff* [2001] ECR I-8691.
340 Ibid para 47.
341 Ibid para 60.
342 'Setting the limits for the implied license in copyright and linking discourse – the European perspective' [2012] IIC 700,702.

III – Possible solutions to the problem

the objective of that rule".[343] The notion is strongly related to the concept of good faith.[344]

This argument, explored earlier, goes: it is against good faith, constitutes contradictory behaviour and defeats the purpose of IPRs to use their blocking effect in certain situations of split ownership of overlaps.[345] If that was the circumstance in several of the analysed scenarios, it is nonetheless true that the application of this doctrine is very much dependent on the specific facts of each case.[346] Furthermore, even in blatant cases of "contradictory behaviour" there might be some reluctance to use this mechanism.[347]

Nonetheless, Axel Metzger[348] rightly points out that there is normative support in articles 8(2) and 41(2) TRIPS and article 3(2) of Directive 2004/48 on the enforcement of intellectual property rights to hold that under certain conditions (such as the one under scrutiny) the doctrine of abuse might trump the exercise of IPRs.

4. Expanding copyright-internal solutions by analogy

Although there are no provisions regulating inter-IPRs conflicts of ownership, some regimes, most notably copyright and patents, have mechanisms to deal with conflicts resulting from joint ownership.[349] Often this is also achieved by applying the general rules of private law on common property or common tenancy.[350]

---

343 (n 160) 1122.
344 Ibid 1145 ff; In IP the concept is used v.g. in the trade mark context (52 (1)(b) CTMR). The interpretation by the CJEU has been quite demanding, see Cases C-529/07 *Lindt* [2009] ECR I-04893 and C-320/12 *Malaysia* (CJEU 27 June 2013). On the rule in detail see A Tsoutsanis, *Trade mark registrations in bad faith* (OUP 2010).
345 F Verkade (n 19) 75.
346 Ibid ("...could in certain circumstances..."). See also the CJEU in *Malaysia* (n 344) at para 36 ("...in order to determine the existence of bad faith, it is necessary to carry out an overall assessment, taking into account all the factors relevant to the particular case...").
347 See n 201.
348 'Abuse of Law in EC Private Law: A (re-)construction from fragments' in R de La Feria and S Vogenauer (eds), *Prohibition of Abuse of Law: A New General Principle in EC Law?* (Hart Publishing 2010) 235, 245.
349 See n 107.
350 Ibid.

B. A general solution?

As Antoon Quaedvlieg[351] puts it "...cases of negative convergence will not always result in simple allowing one regime to take priority over another. Their effects can be much more subtle and sophisticated. For example, the weight of the core regime can result in the provisions of other regimes being subject to a different interpretation."

In this section I shall consider the applicability of copyright specific solutions to the split ownership problem of overlaps by means of analogy. I do not regard patent provisions as a possible general solution since the potential of cumulation for patents is rather low[352] and there are more sensibilities regarding copyright that need to be accommodated.

a) On Analogy

Whenever there is a loophole in the law, an unforeseen situation which requires intervention of the law, legal doctrine speaks of gaps or *lacunae* (*Lücken* in German).[353] Claus-Wilhem Canaris defined it as "incompleteness contrary to the plan of the positive law (i.e. the law within the inner limits of the possible meaning of its text and customary law)".[354] The means to fill these gaps or *lacunae* rely mainly on analogy.[355]

There is a deep debate among legal philosophers on the extent to which these happen.[356] It can be said that legal reasoning somehow differs among

---

351 'Concurrence' (n 9) 30.
352 E Derclaye and M Leistner (n10) 89 ff.
353 On the topic see *inter alia* R Dworkin, 'On Gaps in the Law' in P Amselek and N MacCormick (eds), *Controversies about Law's Ontology* (Edinburgh University Press 1991) 84-90; C-W Canaris, *Die Festsetllung von Lücken im Gesetz* (2nd edn, Dunckner & Humboldt 1983) and K Larenz, *Methodenlehre der Rechtswissenschaft* (6th edn, Springer 1991) 401 ff.
354 Ibid, 30: "Eine Lücke ist eine planwidrige Unvollständigkeit des positive Rechts (d.h. des Gesetzes innerhalb der Grenzen seines möglichen Wortsinnes und des Gewohnheitrechts)".
355 There is a distinction between intra-systematic processes (out of which analogy is paramount) and extra-systematic interventions, such as relying on equity, administrative decision or legislative action.
356 For a good summary of the deductivism and inductivism approaches and defending that not even deductivism presupposes a gapless law, see N MacCormick, *Rhetoric and the Rule of Law – A theory of Legal Reasoning* (OUP 2005) 52 ff.

III – Possible solutions to the problem

common lawyers (who, when applying precedent, reason by analogy)[357] and civil lawyers (who usually depart from codified law and employ analogy mainly as a means to fill the gaps of the statute).[358] Nonetheless both systems are faced with scenarios which demand a legal answer although such an answer is not directly given.[359] It can be added that, whenever a civil lawyer reasons on the basis of precedent or a common lawyer interprets statute, their methodologies might to a certain extent converge or even swap.

The first challenge in dealing with these situations lies in identifying them. There are cases in which the law is silent on the matter precisely because it chose to do so. Leaving the matter unregulated was a conscious and deliberate choice.[360] Then, there is there is no gap, it's a space "free from the law".[361]

Other instances occur when the law bars the use of analogy, as regarding criminal sanctions, tax incidence and other limitations of fundamental rights.[362] No matter how logical it might seem to extend the law to those

---

357 D Hunter, 'Reason is too large: Analogy and precedent in law' 50 Emory Law Journal (2001) 1197, 1222. This is contested by F Schauer, 'Why Precedent in Law (and Elsewhere) is Not Totally (or Even Substantially) about Analogy' KSG Working Paper No. RWP07-036 (2007) 3 <http://ssrn.com/abstract=1747148> ("An argument from precedent does require an initial determination of relevant similarity, but from there the paths diverge, and the typical use of precedent, especially by judges, bears far less affinity to analogical reasoning than most psychologists and perhaps even some lawyers appear to believe").

358 J Holland and J Webb, *Learning Legal Rules* (7th edn, OUP 2010) 381; K Langenbucher, 'Argument by Analogy in European Law' 57 (2008) Cambridge Law Journal 481, 482 ff.

359 This is to be distinguished from the necessary interpretation of general terms that always happens due to the open texture of the law (see e.g. H Hart, *The concept of law* (3rd edn, OUP 2012) 126 ff.). Nonetheless, it should be noted that the difference between extending the scope of the text to encompass new situations and going into analogy is just one of degree.

360 Karl Larenz calls this an "eloquent silence" (*Beredetes Schweigen*) (n353) at 370. K Langenbucher (n358) 485 ("…the mere fact that a novel case does not fall under a role in the Code does not in itself entail the conclusion that there is a gap."). Such a reasoning was used e.g. in Case 30/88 *Hellenic Republic v Commission* [1989] ECR I-3711 AG Opinion of AG Tesauro para 19.

361 C-W Canaris (n353) 40-44.

362 K Langenbucher (n358) 486.

situations, reasoning by analogy is not allowed.[363] Thus, the gap is left unfilled.

If one has identified a (real) gap and there is no impediment to analogy, the next step will be identifying a similar case which has a defined solution in the law and, on the basis of that similarity, extend the application of such solution in order to fill in the gap. It should be stressed that this determination of similarity has always to be done with the *ratio legis* in mind.[364] One needs to interpret the law in order to find out why it contains a certain command and, only after such an interpretation has been done, can one ascertain if the case at hand bears or not the similarity that justifies analogy.[365]

Sometimes it is not possible to find a comparable solution in the law and, as the judge cannot excuse himself from deciding,[366] the Court will have to create a legal solution for the case. But even then the idea is that the legal solution to create is to be taken from the system, to establish a rule as the legislator would have established.

When one extends the application of a single norm to a case, it is said to be *analogia legis* (*Gesetzanalogie*), in case there is the need to create a rule, building on legal principles, then it is called *analogia iuris* (*Rechtanalogie*).[367]

In the situation under analysis, there is an unforeseen situation which requires the intervention of the law. It is unforeseen for no specific regulation of ownership in the case of overlaps is found in statutes. Although some channelling provisions partially avoid overlapping protection, these do not

---

363 A much debated issue (with different outcomes in different jurisdictions) was whether the taking of electricity amounted to theft and if the prohibition of analogy in criminal law barred it. On the topic see C W Maris, 'Milking the Meter.' in P Nerhot (ed), *Legal Knowledge and Analogy* (Springer1991) 71-106.
364 Ibid 488. Article 10(2) of the Portuguese Civil Code puts it rather clear, stating: "There is analogy whenever the justifying reasons for the solution found in the law are also to be found in the unforeseen case". This was inspired by art. 1 of the Swiss Civil Code.
365 As follows from the definition given by Canaris, the difference between analogy and interpretation is the text of the law. If the solution can still be found in the text, it is interpretation, if not then we enter the realm of lacunae and its filling, C-W Canaris (n353) 197.
366 N Luhmann, *Law as a Social System* (OUP 2004) 281. *Non liquet* as a reason not to decide only occurs in international law (cf. P Weil, 'The Court Cannot Conclude Definitively...Non Liquet Revisited' (1997) 36 Columbia Journal of Transnational Law 109).
367 C W Maris (n363) 71, 75-79. J Holland and J Webb (n358) 382.

III – Possible solutions to the problem

ban overlaps and there are provisions in the law that specifically allow it.[368] It is submitted that the situation is problematic and there was no intention to leave it unregulated. Furthermore, this is not a space outside the realm of law. The problem exists precisely due to imperfect interaction of the existing laws.

It can be argued that a proposal that extends copyright solutions by analogy can represent a limitation of the IPR of these people and limitations, as exceptions, should be limited to the minimum and respect the three-step test.[369] Additionally, it can be argued that there should not be room for analogy in exceptional cases.

This whole construction does not seem to hold true. The only question to be answered is whether, according to the *ratio legis* of a certain legal solution one considers applying by analogy, there is room for due differentiation or, on the other hand, the situation under analysis fits well and is similar, in its relevant aspects, to the situation explicitly considered by the lawmaker. If the latter is verified then one can proceed with the analogy. One good way of measuring the solution is considering how it works and whether the results achieved seem fair and sensible.

b) Connected works

As seen, connected works are works which, albeit independent, are combined for joint exploitation.[370] The situation envisaged is slightly different from the problem in hand. In the overlap situation there is no act of combination and the different IPRs are not independent, i.e. capable of separate exploitation. But there also significant commonalities: the use of the combined object is only possible in common and each of the authors has the power to prevent exploitation. Since the commercial interest will often lie only in the exploitation of the common object[371] such difference plays no significant role.

---

368 See supra **III.B.1.**
369 About the test in detail cf. M Senftleben, *Copyright, Limitations and the Three-step Test* (Kluwer Law International 2004).
370 See **I.B.2.b)2**.
371 Which has an "unitary artistic effect, stronger than the sum of the combined works", E Ulmer (n 61) 194.

B. A general solution?

The solutions found in the national legislation seem to provide a good basis for solving conflicts. The German solution, relying on good faith, allows for a great deal of flexibility.[372] The Italian solution promotes legal certainty in the cases where it designates the "prevailing" work.[373] When applying such solution by analogy, although a similar reasoning is possible, it faces most of the obstacles of the prevalence approach.[374] It is nonetheless better in comparison because, unlike prevalence, it safeguards the interests of the "eschewed" owner, which will still be entitled to payment. This represents the equivalent to a compulsory licence or a levy. The "eschewed" owner's right in that situation is reduced to a remuneration right.

c) Joint works

The qualification of joint works requires a tighter collaboration.[375] This is also due to the impossibility of exploiting each author's contribution separately. It is precisely this aspect that renders the concept of joint works particularly suitable to regulate the phenomenon of split ownership in cases of overlaps.[376] Even in face of those situations where unanimity is still required[377] there are mechanisms in place, such as court mediation, to overcome the blocking situation.

It must be added that in several jurisdictions there will be no real difference concerning joint works and connected works, since their respective regimes will lead anyhow to the general rules of private law on common property, common tenancy[378] or joint collaboration.[379] Applying the general rules of civil law might be another way of achieving a similar result. As said by Peukert[380] "the specific problem posed by joint ownership pertains to internal disputes. The necessity to agree on a mode of exploitation increases

---

372 § 9 UrhG.
373 Arts. 33-37 ItalCa, see n 122 .
374 See **III.B**.
375 At least under the adopted definition (at **I.B.2.b) 1**).
376 S Chalton seems to suggest it, howbeit implicitly (n 262) at 181.
377 T Margoni and M Perry (n 122) 32 call it "the anticommons threat".
378 K Garnett, G Davies and G Harbottle (n 132) 333. This is the case in Portugal by article 15 PTCA.
379 As in the German case (see n 118).
380 (n 44) 214.

III – Possible solutions to the problem

transaction costs and can prevent desirable uses. Therefore, the law should help to coordinate the internal operations of the group".

IV – Conclusion

As we have seen, there are no specific rules governing overlaps. The potential for different ownerships is high and most frequently these situations are not regulated by explicit contractual provisions. Beyond the mutual blocking situations, applying the priority in time principle can lead to unfair and difficult results. That's why a different number of strategies might and have been used.

This problem can be tackled by means of interpretation or analogy. The use of general concepts of private law such as implied contract/authorization and abuse of law/estoppel – the ultimate stronghold of every lawyer – faces some obstacles in the present legal framework.

Extending copyright solutions by analogy seems thus to be the best option in face of the law as it stands. Nonetheless, a combination of these methodologies is to be expected and should be explored.

It is submitted that it would be useful to have general provisions dealing with overlaps and particularly one addressing this problem. In the absence of a general regulation of overlaps, this rule can be systematically placed either on copyright ownership rules – preventing the different ownership or deeming the joint works/connected works solutions applicable to the problem – or as a limitation to the scope of rights – reducing them to a mutual remuneration right.[381]

According to the latter solution, either of the overlapping IPRs owner's would be able to exploit the object independently and would owe the other his share of the profits, presumed equal. This can obviously lead to discussions – which are not alien to IP; for instance when it comes to damage calculation – on how much of a profit is due to a specific IPR and how much is a result of other efforts, investment and intangibles.[382] That is indeed discussing a wider and more fundamental question: how relevant is Intellectual Property?

---

381 This has an equivalent effect to statutory cross-licensing. The solution is already found v.g. in art. 18(1) PTCA regarding connected works.
382 This is why B E Cookson (n 3) writes that a business has only one goodwill.

Annex

Annex I: The interface of designs and copyright under Russian law[*]

Under Russian Law, works of applied art can be protected both under copyright and design patents.[383] There seems to be no single filtering requirement,[384] but the system cannot be characterized as one of full cumulation.[385] Pavel Savitsky briefly describes case law as inconsistent; some decisions requiring registration for copyright protection and other relying on a teleological notion of IPRs (right A for x and right B for y).[386]

The interface between the two types of protection in matters of enforcement was clarified by the Resolution of the Plenum of the Supreme Court.[387] According to paragraph 24 of the Resolution, if the object of the author's rights is registered, **with the consent of the right holder**, as an

---

[*] The translations of the Russian language are the work of Daria Kim, LLM. IP, to whom I express my gratitude not only for that but also for having brought this decision to my attention and elucidating me on several aspects of Russian law.

[383] Article 1259 (1) of the Civil Code of the Russian Federation lists works of graphics, design and other works of visual arts as the subject matter of author's rights. The Part IV of the Civil Code of the Russian regulates intellectual property. It came into force as of January 1, 2008. An English unofficial translation can be found on the website of the Federal Service for Intellectual Property (Rospatent) <http://www.rupto.ru/rupto/nfile/3b05468f-4b25-11e1-36f8-9c8e9921fb2c/Civil_Code.pdf.> accessed 29 August 2013.

[384] Elaborating on the current criteria see P Savitsky, 'Protection of product appearance in Russia' [2013] EIPR 143, 146.

[385] Pursuant to paragraph 1 of Art. 1357 of the Civil Code of the RF, the author of the industrial design has the right to obtain the patent for industrial design. According to paragraph 2 of the same article, the contract for assignment of the right to obtain patent for industrial design has to be concluded in the written form, otherwise it shall be void. There are special rules regarding rights ownership in industrial designs created within employment duties (Art. 1370 of the RF Civil Code) ; under commissioning contract (Art. 1372) and under municipal and government contracts (Art. 1373).

[386] (n 384) 148.

[387] The Resolution of the Plenum of the Supreme Court of the Russian Federation and the Supreme Commercial Court of the Russian Federation No. 5/29 of March 26, 2009 "On Certain Questions Arising in Relation to the Enactment of the Fourth Part of the Civil Code of the Russian Federation.".

Annex

industrial design, the means of enforcement of the exclusive rights shall depend on the nature of the infringement (emphasis added) .[388]

If cumulation occurs and the plaintiff claims protection from both regimes in the same action one distinction will be drawn. In particular, if the alleged infringer performs actions using the industrial design by means affecting exclusive rights in the industrial design, the plaintiff can only invoke industrial design rights. In case of the violation of exclusive rights in the copyrighted work by means not related to the use of the industrial design, the copyright holder can invoke her exclusive right.

The boundary between acts that only are copyright infringement and not design infringement is very hard to draw and the Resolution provides no guidance in this respect. Even though copyright and design deal with commercial exploitation, the difference might lie in the mass reproduction (design-type infringement) vs. "plagiarism"/isolated copying (copyright-kind).[389] Even if that is a distinction that might have some bearing in applied arts if we think of copyright in books, music or computer programs it loses its meaning as these works also aim at mass reproduction.[390]

---

[388] In particular, if the alleged infringer performs actions using the industrial design by means prohibited under Article 1358 of the RF Civil Code, a patent holder can invoke industrial design rights in accordance with Articles 1406, 1407, and 1252 of the RF Civil Code. In case of a violation of exclusive rights in a work as provided under Article 1270 of the RF Civil Code, by means not involving the use of the patented industrial design incorporated in the work at issue, the copyright holder can invoke the rights according to the rules and procedures provided under Articles 1301 and 1252 of the RF Civil Code.

[389] This is the criterion used in the United Kingdom but, as noted, there are several criteria used to make the distinction between the two areas, such as artistic nature, artistic merit, form of reproduction, etc. Reasoning on a similar basis see A Quaedvlieg, 'Concurrence and Convergence in Industrial Design: 3-Dimensional Shapes Excluded by Trademark Law' in W Grosheide and J Brinkhof (eds) , *Articles on Crossing Borders Borders between traditional and actual Intellectual Property Law* (Intersentia 2004) 23, 39 ("the character of the work and the mode of exploitation") .

[390] S. 52 CDPA and The Copyright (Industrial Process and Excluded Articles) (No. 2) Order 1989 (providing: "An article is to be regarded for the purposes of section 52 of the Act (...) as made by an industrial process ift is one of more than fifty articles") . Precisely because of such objection the Order excludes "printed matter primarily of a literary or artistic character, including book jackets, calendars, certificates, coupons, dress-making patterns, greetings cards, labels, leaflets, maps, plans, playing cards, postcards, stamps, trade advertisements, trade forms and cards, transfers and similar articles.".

Annex I: The interface of designs and copyright under Russian law

Design law scope is wider than copyright, as its protection is objective, there is no need to prove copying.[391] There are, nonetheless, certain actions covered by copyright and not by design law.[392] For instance, most copyright laws, including Russian law, establish moral rights[393] that give the author[394] certain powers and prerogatives. Moreover, the reproduction of a 3-d design in two dimensions is clear copyright infringement, whereas it constitutes a debatable issue in the case of designs.[395]

What seems to result from the Resolution is: in the overlapping area design patents prevail. But that prevalence does not preempt copyright in the design because there are other areas where there is no overlap. And in those areas copyright exists and might act without being hindered by design law.

The Resolution is silent in the matter of exceptions but they seem to have to be considered only in the context of the applicable regime. If the infringement is characterized as "design-type" and is later excused under a certain design specific defence, it does not seem possible for the owner to claim copyright additionally.

This constitutes an example of prevalence.[396] The Resolution of the Plenum of the Russian Supreme Court does not address directly the ownership problem but mentions the consent of the right holder. As the applicant for a design patent needs not to prove entitlement[397] this does not filter legitimacy of ownership. It is also not clear what are the consequences of a

---

391 Art. 1229 of the RF Civil Code defines exclusive rights for all types of intellectual property. To compare the scope of exclusive rights in artistic works and industrial designs, see Articles 1270 and 1358 of the RF Civil Code.
392 P Savitsky, (n 384) 144.
393 Russian law follows the European continental *droit d' auteur* tradition and provides for moral rights. Like the CDR, Russian law has a paternity right, i.e., the right to be recognized as the author of the invention, utility model and industrial design for the designer. This right cannot be assigned/transferred. (See Art. 1356 of the RF Civil Code) .
394 Or her successor in title in the rare countries where assignment of moral rights is possible.
395 See the decision of the BGH *Deutschebahn v Fraunhofer* with a favourable annotation by H Hartwig [2011] GRUR 1117.
396 See **III.B.2**.
397 According to the paragraph 5.1. of the Administrative regulation of the Federal Service for Intellectual Property, Patents and Trademarks regarding application, examination and granting patents of the Russian Federation for industrial designs (Annex to the Order of the Ministry of Education and Science of the Russian Federation of October 29, 2008 No. 325) , the applicant does not need to provide a document proving the right to obtain the patent.

registration without the consent of the right owner. Most likely he will be able to claim entitlement to the design patent, pursuant to art. 1357(1) Civil Code of the RF.

Annex II: Selected Legislative Provisions

The provisions presented are those cited in the text and which are not of usual access. Therefore international treaties, directives and regulations in force are not shown. Unless otherwise noted the translation are the author's responsibility.

UK Copyright, Designs and Patents Act 1988

9 Authorship of work.

(1) In this Part "author", in relation to a work, means the person who creates it.
(2) That person shall be taken to be—
(aa) in the case of a sound recording, the producer;
(ab) in the case of a film, the producer and the principal director;
(b) in the case of a broadcast, the person making the broadcast (see section 6(3)) or, in the case of a broadcast which relays another broadcast by reception and immediate re-transmission, the person making that other broadcast;
(c) ………………..
(d) in the case of the typographical arrangement of a published edition, the publisher.
(3) In the case of a literary, dramatic, musical or artistic work which is computer-generated, the author shall be taken to be the person by whom the arrangements necessary for the creation of the work are undertaken.
(…)

10 Works of joint authorship.

(1) In this Part a "work of joint authorship" means a work produced by the collaboration of two or more authors in which the contribution of each author is not distinct from that of the other author or authors.

(1A) A film shall be treated as a work of joint authorship unless the producer and the principal director are the same person.
(2) A broadcast shall be treated as a work of joint authorship in any case where more than one person is to be taken as making the broadcast (see section 6(3)).
(3) References in this Part to the author of a work shall, except as otherwise provided, be construed in relation to a work of joint authorship as references to all the authors of the work.

11 First ownership of copyright.

(1) The author of a work is the first owner of any copyright in it, subject to the following provisions.
(2) Where a literary, dramatic, musical or artistic work or a film, is made by an employee in the course of his employment, his employer is the first owner of any copyright in the work subject to any agreement to the contrary.
(3) This section does not apply to Crown copyright or Parliamentary copyright (see sections 163 and 165) or to copyright which subsists by virtue of section 168 (copyright of certain international organisations) .
(…)

51 Design documents and models.

(1) It is not an infringement of any copyright in a design document or model recording or embodying a design for anything other than an artistic work or a typeface to make an article to the design or to copy an article made to the design.
(2) Nor is it an infringement of the copyright to issue to the public, or include in a film or communicate to the public, anything the making of which was, by virtue of subsection (1) , not an infringement of that copyright.
(3) In this section—
"design" means the design of any aspect of the shape or configuration (whether internal or external) of the whole or part of an article, other than surface decoration; and
"design document" means any record of a design, whether in the form of a drawing, a written description, a photograph, data stored in a computer or otherwise.

52 Effect of exploitation of design derived from artistic work.

(1) This section applies where an artistic work has been exploited, by or with the licence of the copyright owner, by—

(a) making by an industrial process articles falling to be treated for the purposes of this Part as copies of the work, and
(b) marketing such articles, in the United Kingdom or elsewhere.
(2) After the end of the period of 25 years from the end of the calendar year in which such articles are first marketed, the work may be copied by making articles of any description, or doing anything for the purpose of making articles of any description, and anything may be done in relation to articles so made, without infringing copyright in the work.
(3) Where only part of an artistic work is exploited as mentioned in subsection (1), subsection (2) applies only in relation to that part.
(4) The Secretary of State may by order make provision—
(a) as to the circumstances in which an article, or any description of article, is to be regarded for the purposes of this section as made by an industrial process;
(b) excluding from the operation of this section such articles of a primarily literary or artistic character as he thinks fit.
(5) An order shall be made by statutory instrument which shall be subject to annulment in pursuance of a resolution of either House of Parliament.
(6) In this section—
(a) references to articles do not include films; and
(b) references to the marketing of an article are to its being sold or let for hire or offered or exposed for sale or hire.
(…)

173 Construction of references to copyright owner.

(1) Where different persons are (whether in consequence of a partial assignment or otherwise) entitled to different aspects of copyright in a work, the copyright owner for any purpose of this Part is the person who is entitled to the aspect of copyright relevant for that purpose.
(2) Where copyright (or any aspect of copyright) is owned by more than one person jointly, references in this Part to the copyright owner are to all the owners, so that, in particular, any requirement of the licence of the copyright owner requires the licence of all of them.

The Copyright (Industrial Process and Excluded Articles) (No. 2) Order 1989

(...)
2. An article is to be regarded for the purposes of section 52 of the Act (limitation of copyright protection for design derived from artistic work) as made by an industrial process if—
(a) it is one of more than fifty articles which—
(i) all fall to be treated for the purposes of Part I of the Act as copies of a particular artistic work, but
(ii) do not all together constitute a single set of articles as defined in section 44(1) of the Registered Designs Act 1949; or
(b) it consists of goods manufactured in lengths or pieces, not being hand-made goods.
3.—(1) There are excluded from the operation of section 52 of the Act—
(a) works of sculpture, other than casts or models used or intended to be used as models or patterns to be multiplied by any industrial process;
(b) wall plaques, medals and medallions; and
(c) printed matter primarily of a literary or artistic character, including book jackets, calendars, certificates, coupons, dress-making patterns, greetings cards, labels, leaflets, maps, plans, playing cards, postcards, stamps, trade advertisements, trade forms and cards, transfers and similar articles.
(2) Nothing in article 2 of this Order shall be taken to limit the meaning of "industrial process" in paragraph (1) (a) of this article.

Ireland Copyright and Related Rights Act, 2000

23.—(1) The author of a work shall be the first owner of the copyright unless—

(a) the work is made by an employee in the course of employment, in which case the employer is the first owner of any copyright in the work, subject to any agreement to the contrary,
(b) the work is the subject of Government or Oireachtas copyright,
(c) the work is the subject of the copyright of a prescribed international organisation, or
(d) the copyright in the work is conferred on some other person by an enactment.

Annex

(2) Where a work, other than a computer program, is made by an author in the course of employment by the proprietor of a newspaper or periodical, the author may use the work for any purpose, other than for the purposes of making available that work to newspapers or periodicals, without infringing the copyright in the work.

Austrian Copyright Act

§ 10. (1) Urheber eines Werkes ist, wer es geschaffen hat. (…)	Section 10. (1) The author of the work is the person who created it. (…)
Miturheber. § 11. (1) Haben mehrere gemeinsam ein Werk geschaffen, bei dem die Ergebnisse ihres Schaffens eine untrennbare Einheit bilden, so steht das Urheberrecht allen Miturhebern gemeinschaftlich zu.	**Co-authors** Section 11. (1) When more than one person has created a work so that the result constitutes and indivisible unity, copyright belongs jointly to all co-authors.
(2) Jeder Miturheber ist für sich berechtigt, Verletzungen des Urheberrechtes gerichtlich zu verfolgen. Zu einer Änderung oder Verwertung des Werkes bedarf es des Einverständnisses aller Miturheber. Verweigert ein Miturheber seine Einwilligung ohne ausreichenden Grund, so kann ihn jeder andere Miturheber auf deren Erteilung klagen. (…)	(2) Each co-author can by himself enforce the copyright. To modify or exploit the work the consent of all co-authors is required. In case of denial without sufficient reasons, each co-author can sue the remainder for consent. (…)
(3) Die Verbindung von Werken verschiedener Art – wie die eines Werkes der Tonkunst mit einem Sprachwerk oder einem Filmwerk – begründet an sich keine Miturheberschaft. (…)	(3) The combination of works of a different type – like a work of music with a literary work or a film – does not imply co-authorship. (…)

Übertragung des Urheberrechtes. § 23. (1) Das Urheberrecht ist vererblich; in Erfüllung einer auf den Todesfall getroffenen Anordnung kann es auch auf Sondernachfolger übertragen werden. (…)	Transfer of Copyright Section 23. (1) Copyright is hereditable; it can also be transferred by special testamentary disposition. (…)
(3) Im übrigen ist das Urheberrecht unübertragbar.	(3) Otherwise, copyright is unassignable.
(4) Geht das Urheberrecht auf mehrere Personen über, so sind auf sie die für Miturheber (§ 11) geltenden Vorschriften entsprechend anzuwenden.	(4) If the copyright is transferred to more than one person, the rules regarding co-authorship are applicable with the necessary adaptions.

German Copyright Act[398]

§ 7 Urheber Urheber ist der Schöpfer des Werkes.	Section 7 Author The author is the creator of the work.
§ 8 Miturheber (1) Haben mehrere ein Werk gemeinsam geschaffen, ohne daß sich ihre Anteile gesondert verwerten lassen, so sind sie Miturheber des Werkes.	Section 8 Joint authors (1) If several persons have jointly created a work that is not seperatley (individually) exploitable, they are joint authors of the work.
(2) Das Recht zur Veröffentlichung und zur Verwertung des Werkes steht den Miturhebern zur gesamten Hand zu; Änderungen des Werkes sind nur mit Einwilligung der Miturheber zulässig. Ein Miturheber darf jedoch seine Einwilligung zur Veröffentlichung, Verwertung oder Änderung nicht wider Treu und Glauben verweigern. Jeder Miturheber ist berechtigt, Ansprüche aus Verletzungen des gemeinsamen	(2) The right of publication and of exploitation of the work is owned jointly by the joint authors; alterations to the work shall be permissible only with the consent of the joint authors. However, a joint author may not refuse his consent to publication, exploitation or alteration contrary to the principles of good faith. Each joint author shall be entitled to assert claims arising from violations of the joint copyright; he may, however,

---

398 A translation by Ute Reusch can be found at http://www.gesetze-im-internet.de/englisch_urhg/index.html. The translation provided here is however mine.

Urheberrechts geltend zu machen; er kann jedoch nur Leistung an alle Miturheber verlangen.

(3) Die Erträgnisse aus der Nutzung des Werkes gebühren den Miturhebern nach dem Umfang ihrer Mitwirkung an der Schöpfung des Werkes, wenn nichts anderes zwischen den Miturhebern vereinbart ist.

(4) Ein Miturheber kann auf seinen Anteil an den Verwertungsrechten (§ 15) verzichten. Der Verzicht ist den anderen Miturhebern gegenüber zu erklären. Mit der Erklärung wächst der Anteil den anderen Miturhebern zu.

§ 9 Urheber verbundener Werke
Haben mehrere Urheber ihre Werke zu gemeinsamer Verwertung miteinander verbunden, so kann jeder vom anderen die Einwilligung zur Veröffentlichung, Verwertung und Änderung der verbundenen Werke verlangen, wenn die Einwilligung dem anderen nach Treu und Glauben zuzumuten ist.

§ 29 Rechtsgeschäfte über das Urheberrecht
(1) Das Urheberrecht ist nicht übertragbar, es sei denn, es wird in Erfüllung einer Verfügung von Todes wegen oder an Miterben im Wege der Erbauseinandersetzung übertragen.
(...)

§ 31 Einräumung von Nutzungsrechten
Entsprechendes gilt für die Frage, ob ein Nutzungsrecht eingeräumt wird, ob es sich um ein einfaches oder ausschließliches Nutzungsrecht handelt, wie weit Nutzungsrecht und Verbotsrecht reichen und welchen

demand performance only to all of the joint authors.

(3) Profits resulting from the use of the work are due to the joint authors in accordance to the extent of their involvement in the creation of the work, unless otherwise agreed between the joint authors.

(4) A joint author may waive his share of the exploitation rights (Article 15). He shall make a declaration of waiver to the other joint authors. Upon his declaration his share shall accrue.

Section 9 Authors of connected works
Where several authors have combined their works for the purpose of joint exploitation, each may require the consent of the others to the publication, exploitation or alteration of the compound works if the consent of the others may be reasonably expected in good faith.

Section 29 Transactions regarding copyright
(1) Copyright is not assignable unless in execution of a testamentary disposition or to co-heirs as part of the partition of an estate.
(...)

Section 31 Grant of exploitation rights
corresponding rule shall apply to the questions of whether an exploitation right has in fact been granted, whether it shall be a non-exclusive or an exclusive exploitation right, how far the exploitation right and the right to forbid extent, and to what limitations the exploitation right shall be subject.

Einschränkungen das Nutzungsrecht unterliegt.	
§ 43 Urheber in Arbeits- oder Dienstverhältnissen Die Vorschriften dieses Unterabschnitts sind auch anzuwenden, wenn der Urheber das Werk in Erfüllung seiner Verpflichtungen aus einem Arbeits- oder Dienstverhältnis geschaffen hat, soweit sich aus dem Inhalt oder dem Wesen des Arbeits- oder Dienstverhältnisses nichts anderes ergibt.	**Section 43 Authors in employment or service relation** The provisions of this Subsection are applicable if the author has created the work in the fulfilment of duties resulting from an employment or service relationship, unless it results otherwise from the terms or nature of the employment or service relationship.
§ 69b Urheber in Arbeits- und Dienstverhältnissen (1) Wird ein Computerprogramm von einem Arbeitnehmer in Wahrnehmung seiner Aufgaben oder nach den Anweisungen seines Arbeitgebers geschaffen, so ist ausschließlich der Arbeitgeber zur Ausübung aller vermögensrechtlichen Befugnisse an dem Computerprogramm berechtigt, sofern nichts anderes vereinbart ist.	**Article 69b Authors in employment or service relation** (1) If a computer program is created by an employee in the execution of his duties or following instructions by his employer, the employer is exclusively entitled to exercise all economic rights in the computer program, unless otherwise agreed.
(2) Absatz 1 ist auf Dienstverhältnisse entsprechend anzuwenden. (…)	(2) Paragraph (1) applies mutatis mutandis to service relationships. (…)
(5) Sind bei der Einräumung eines Nutzungsrechts die Nutzungsarten nicht ausdrücklich einzeln bezeichnet, so bestimmt sich nach dem von beiden Partnern zugrunde gelegten Vertragszweck, auf welche Nutzungsarten es sich erstreckt.	(5) If the types of exploitation have not been specifically designated when an exploitation right was granted, the types of use to which the right extends shall be determined in accordance with the purpose envisaged by both parties to the contract. A

Annex

French Intellectual Property Code

Article L111-1	**L-111-1**
L'auteur d'une oeuvre de l'esprit jouit sur cette oeuvre, du seul fait de sa création, d'un droit de propriété incorporelle exclusif et opposable à tous. Ce droit comporte des attributs d'ordre intellectuel et moral ainsi que des attributs d'ordre patrimonial, qui sont déterminés par les livres Ier et III du présent code. L'existence ou la conclusion d'un contrat de louage d'ouvrage ou de service par l'auteur d'une oeuvre de l'esprit n'emporte pas dérogation à la jouissance du droit reconnu par le premier alinéa, sous réserve des exceptions prévues par le présent code. Sous les mêmes réserves, il n'est pas non plus dérogé à la jouissance de ce même droit lorsque l'auteur de l'oeuvre de l'esprit est un agent de l'Etat, d'une collectivité territoriale, d'un établissement public à caractère administratif, d'une autorité administrative indépendante dotée de la personnalité morale ou de la Banque de France. (…)	The author of an intellectual work enjoys, by the mere fact of its creation, a right of intellectual property exclusive and opposable to everyone. That right comprises attributes of moral and intellectual nature as well as the ones of economic nature that are established in the first and third chapters of the present Code. The existence or the signing of a commissioning or labour contract by the author does not imply any derogation of the right recognised in the first paragraph, unless otherwise provided in the code. Under the same conditions that right is also not affected when the author is a State agent or worker of a local entity or a public establishment of administrative nature, of an independent administrative authority with legal personality or the Bank of France. (…)
Article L113-2	**L – 113-2**
Est dite de collaboration l'oeuvre à la création de laquelle ont concouru plusieurs personnes physiques. Est dite composite l'oeuvre nouvelle à laquelle est incorporée une oeuvre préexistante sans la collaboration de l'auteur de cette dernière. Est dite collective l'oeuvre créée sur l'initiative d'une personne physique ou morale qui l'édite, la publie et la divulgue sous sa direction et son nom et dans laquelle la contribution personnelle	The work in whose creation several natural persons took part is called a collaborative work. The new work which incorporates a previous work without the collaboration of the author of the former is called a composite work. The work created by the initiative of a legal or natural person that edits it, publishes it and discloses it under its direction and name and in which the personal contributions of the several

des divers auteurs participant à son élaboration se fond dans l'ensemble en vue duquel elle est conçue, sans qu'il soit possible d'attribuer à chacun d'eux un droit distinct sur l'ensemble réalisé.

Article L113-3
L'oeuvre de collaboration est la propriété commune des coauteurs.
Les coauteurs doivent exercer leurs droits d'un commun accord.
En cas de désaccord, il appartient à la juridiction civile de statuer.
Lorsque la participation de chacun des coauteurs relève de genres différents, chacun peut, sauf convention contraire, exploiter séparément sa contribution personnelle, sans toutefois porter préjudice à l'exploitation de l'oeuvre commune

Article L113-4
L'oeuvre composite est la propriété de l'auteur qui l'a réalisée, sous réserve des droits de l'auteur de l'oeuvre préexistante.

Article L113-5
L'oeuvre collective est, sauf preuve contraire, la propriété de la personne physique ou morale sous le nom de laquelle elle est divulguée.
Cette personne est investie des droits de l'auteur.
(…)

Article L132-31
Dans le cas d'une oeuvre de commande utilisée pour la publicité, le contrat entre le producteur et l'auteur entraîne, sauf clause contraire, cession au producteur des droits d'exploitation de l'oeuvre,
(…) .

---

authors that took part in its elaboration is merged in a unity without being possible to attribute each of them a distinct right on the unity created is called a collective work.

L-113-3
The collaborative work is common property of the co-authors.
The co-authors must exercise their rights in mutual agreement.
In case of disagreement, civil court shall rule.
When the contributions of each of the co-authors belongs to different genres, each of them can, unless otherwise agreed, exploit his contribution separately, without however harming the exploitation of the common work

L 113-4
The composite work belongs to the author that has created it, without prejudice to the rights of the author of the previous work.

L-113-5
The collective work, unless proven otherwise, belongs to the legal or natural person under the name of which it is disclosed.
That person owns the copyright.
(…)

L-132-31
In the case of a commissioned work used in advertising, the contract between the producer and the author implies, unless otherwise stated, an assignment to the producer of the exploitation of the work
(…)

Italian Copyright Act

Art. 2. In particolare sono comprese nella protezione: (10) *Le opere del disegno industriale che presentino di per sé carattere creativo e valore artistico.*	**Art 2.** Among others are protected by copyright the: (10) works of industrial design that have creative nature and artistic value.
Art. 3. Le opere collettive, costituite dalla riunione di opere o di parti di opere, che hanno carattere di creazione autonoma, come risultato della scelta e del coordinamento ad un determinato fine letterario, scientifico, didattico, religioso, politico od artistico, quali le enciclopedie, i dizionari, le antologie, le riviste e i giornali, sono protette come opere originali indipendentemente e senza pregiudizio dei diritti di autore sulle opere o sulle parti di opere di cui sono composte.	**Art 3** Collective works, resulting from the gathering of works or part of works, that constitute an autonomous creation, as a result of selection and combination in order to achieve a certain literary, scientific, teaching, religious, political or artistic goal, like encyclopaedias, dictionaries, anthologies, magazines and newspapers, are protected as original works independently and without prejudice to the copyright in the elements that constitute it.
Art. 6. Il titolo originario dell'acquisto del diritto di autore è costituito dalla creazione dell'opera, quale particolare espressione del lavoro intellettuale.	**Art. 6** The original title of copyright is acquired by the creation of the work as a particular expression of intellectual labour.
Art. 7. È considerato autore dell'opera collettiva chi organizza e dirige la creazione dell'opera stessa. (…)	**Art. 7** It is considered the author of a collective work the one who organizes and directs its creation. (…)
Art. 10. Se l'opera è stata creata con il contributo indistinguibile ed inscindibile di più persone, il diritto di autore appartiene in comune a tutti i coautori. Le parti indivise si presumono di valore eguale, salvo la prova per iscritto di diverso accordo.	**Art. 10** If the work has been created with the indistinguishable and indivisible contributions of several persons, the copyright is owned jointly by all co-authors. The undivided parts are presumed to be of equal value, unless otherwise agreed in writing.

Annex II: Selected Legislative Provisions

Sono applicabili le disposizioni che regolano la comunione. La difesa del diritto morale può peraltro essere sempre esercitata individualmente da ciascun coautore e l'opera non può essere pubblicata, se inedita, né può essere modificata o utilizzata in forma diversa da quella della prima pubblicazione, senza l'accordo di tutti i coautori. Tuttavia in caso di ingiustificato rifiuto di uno o più coautori, la pubblicazione, la modificazione o la nuova utilizzazione dell'opera può essere autorizzata dall'autorità giudiziaria, alle condizioni e con le modalità da essa stabilite.	The rules that regulate co-ownership are applicable. Each author can always exercise his moral rights individually and the work cannot be published, if unpublished, cannot be modified or used in a different way than the one according to which it was in its first publication, without the agreement of all the co-authors. However, in case of unjustified refusal by one or more co-authors, the publication, modification or new use of the work can be authorized by the judicial authorities and used accordingly.
Art. 11.	**Art. 11**
Alle amministrazioni dello Stato, alle Province ed ai Comuni, spetta il diritto di autore sulle opere create e pubblicate sotto il loro nome ed a loro conto e spese. Lo stesso diritto spetta agli enti privati che non perseguano scopi di lucro, salvo diverso accordo con gli autori delle opere pubblicate, nonché alle accademie e agli altri enti pubblici culturali sulla raccolta dei loro atti e sulle loro pubblicazioni.	All the State administrations, provinces and communes own the copyright in the works created and published on their behalf and at their expenses. The same applies to the not for profit private entities, unless otherwise agreed with the authors of the published works, and to all universities and other public cultural entities on the collections of their proceedings and publications
Art. 12bis.	**Art 12bis**
Salvo patto contrario, il datore di lavoro è titolare del diritto esclusivo di utilizzazione economica del programma per elaboratore o della banca di dati creati dal lavoratore dipendente nell'esecuzione delle sue mansioni o su istruzioni impartite dallo stesso datore di lavoro. (…)	Unless otherwise agreed, the employer is the owner of an exclusive right of economic use of the computer programs and the databases created by his employee in the context of his employment, according to instructions given by the employer. (…)
Art. 34.	**Art. 34**
L'esercizio dei diritti di utilizzazione economica spetta all'autore della parte	The exercise of the right of economic use belongs to the author of the musical

95

Annex

musicale, salvi tra le parti i diritti derivanti dalla comunione.
Il profitto della utilizzazione economica è ripartito in proporzione del valore del rispettivo contributo letterario o musicale.
Nelle opere liriche si considera che il valore della parte musicale rappresenti la frazione di tre quarti del valore complessivo dell'opera.
Nelle operette, nei melologhi, nelle composizioni musicali con parole, nei balli e balletti musicali, il valore dei due contributi si considera uguale.
Ciascuno dei collaboratori ha diritto di utilizzare separatamente e indipendentemente la propria opera, salvo il disposto degli articoli seguenti.
(...)

Art. 37.
Nelle opere coreografiche o pantomimiche e nelle altre composte di musica, di parole o di danze o di mimica, quali le riviste musicali ed opere simili, in cui la parte musicale non ha funzione o valore principale, l'esercizio dei diritti di utilizzazione economica, salvo patto contrario, spetta all'autore della parte coreografica o pantomimica, e, nelle riviste musicali, all'autore della parte letteraria.
(...)

Sezione II
Opere collettive, riviste e giornali
Art. 38.
Nell'opera collettiva, salvo patto in contrario, il diritto di utilizzazione economica spetta all'editore dell'opera stessa, senza pregiudizio del diritto derivante dall'applicazione dell'art. 7.
Ai singoli collaboratori dell'opera collettiva è riservato il diritto di

part, except for the rights arising out of the joint ownership between the parties. The profits of the economic use are shared according to the value of the literary and musical contribution.
In the lyrical works the contribution of the musical part is considered to be three quarters of the overall value of the work.
In the *operette*, melologues, musical compositions with words, balls and musical ballets, the value of the two contributions is considered the same. Any of the contributors has the right to use his own work separately and independently, except in the cases provided in the following article.
(...)

Art. 37.
In the choreographic or pantomimic works and in other works which have music, words or dance, like the revue and similar works, in which the music does not have the main function or value, the exercise of the rights of economic use, unless otherwise agreed, belong to the author of the choreographic or pantomimic part and, in the musical revue, to the author of the literary part.
(...)

Section II
Collective works, magazines and newspapers
Art. 38.
In the collective work, unless otherwise agreed, the right of economic use belongs to the editor of the work, without prejudice to the right resulting from article 7.

Annex II: Selected Legislative Provisions

utilizzare la propria opera separatamente, con la osservanza dei patti convenuti e, in difetto, delle norme seguenti.	The contributors to the collective work retain the right to use their own work separately, in accordance to what has been established and, in absence of agreement, according to the following rules.

Portuguese Copyright Act

SECÇÃO II **Da atribuição do direito de autor** **Artigo 11.º** **Titularidade** O direito de autor pertence ao criador intelectual da obra, salvo disposição expressa em contrário.	**Section II** **Of copyright ownership** **Art 11** **Ownership** Copyright belongs to the intellectual creator of the work, unless otherwise stated.
Artigo 13.º **Obra subsidiada** Aquele que subsidie ou financie por qualquer forma, total ou parcialmente, a preparação, conclusão, divulgação ou publicação de uma obra não adquire por esse facto sobre esta, salvo convenção escrita em contrário, qualquer dos poderes incluídos no direito de autor.	**Art 13** **Subsidized work** Whoever pays or subsidizes in any way, totally or partially, the preparation, conclusion, disclosure or publication of a work does not, by that reason, unless agreement in writing to the contrary, any copyright.
Artigo 14.º **Determinação da titularidade em casos excepcionais** 1 – Sem prejuízo do disposto no artigo 174.º, a titularidade do direito de autor relativo a obra feita por encomenda ou por conta de outrem, quer em cumprimento de dever funcional quer de contrato de trabalho, determina-se de harmonia com o que tiver sido convencionado. 2 – Na falta de convenção, presume-se que a titularidade do direito de autor relativo a obra feita por conta de outrem pertence ao seu criador intelectual.	**Art. 14** **Determining ownership in exceptional cases** 1 – Without prejudice to article 174, the ownership of copyright either in a commissioned work or a work created in fulfilment of duties arising out of a labour contract is to be determined according to what has been established. 2 – In the absence of agreement, it is presumed that the copyright in work created on request belongs to its creator.

3 – A circunstância de o nome do criador da obra não vir mencionado nesta ou não figurar no local destinado para o efeito segundo o uso universal constitui presunção de que o direito de autor fica a pertencer à entidade por conta de quem a obra é feita.
4 – Ainda quando a titularidade do conteúdo patrimonial do direito de autor pertença àquele para quem a obra é realizada, o seu criador intelectual pode exigir, para além da remuneração ajustada e independentemente do próprio facto da divulgação ou publicação, uma remuneração especial:
a) Quando a criação intelectual exceda claramente o desempenho, ainda que zeloso, da função ou tarefa que lhe estava confiada;
b) Quando da obra vierem a fazer-se utilizações ou a retirar-se vantagens não incluídas nem previstas na fixação da remuneração ajustada.

Artigo 16.º
Noção de obra feita em colaboração e de obra colectiva
1 – A obra que for criação de uma pluralidade de pessoas denomina-se:
a) Obra feita em colaboração, quando divulgada ou publicada em nome dos colaboradores ou de algum deles, quer possam discriminar-se quer não os contributos individuais;
b) Obra colectiva, quando organizada por iniciativa de entidade singular ou colectiva e divulgada ou publicada em seu nome.
2 – A obra de arte aleatória em que a contribuição criativa do ou dos intérpretes se ache originariamente

3 – The absence of the name of the creator according to common usage establishes a presumption that the copyright is owned by the entity for whom the work was created.

4 – Even when the copyright belongs to the entity for whom the work was created, its intellectual creator can demand, on top of the established compensation and independently of disclosure or publication, an equitable remuneration:
a) When the intellectual creation clearly exceeds the performance, even if zealous, of the function or task that was attributed to him;
b) When out of the work's exploitation result advantages that were not foreseen or predicted in the remuneration established.

Art. 16
Definition of collaborative work and collective work
1 – The work created by several people is called:
a) Collaborative work, if it has been disclosed or published under the name of the collaborators or one of them, independently of the possibility to differentiate individual contributions:
b) Collective work, when organized by the initiative of a singular or collective entity and disclosed or published under its name.
2- The aleatory work, in which the creative contribution of one or several interpreters is predicted is considered a collaborative work.

prevista considera-se obra feita em colaboração.

Artigo 17.º
Obra feita em colaboração

1 – O direito de autor de obra feita em colaboração, na sua unidade, pertence a todos os que nela tiverem colaborado, aplicando-se ao exercício comum desse direito as regras de compropriedade.
2 – Salvo estipulação em contrário, que deve ser sempre reduzida a escrito, consideram-se de valor igual às partes indivisas dos autores na obra feita em colaboração.
3 – Se a obra feita em colaboração for divulgada ou publicada apenas em nome de algum ou alguns dos colaboradores, presume-se, na falta de designação explícita dos demais em qualquer parte da obra, que os não designados cederam os seus direitos àquele ou àqueles em nome de quem a divulgação ou publicação é feita.
(…)

Artigo 18.º
Direitos individuais dos autores de obra feita em colaboração

1 – Qualquer dos autores pode solicitar a divulgação, a publicação, a exploração ou a modificação de obra feita em colaboração, sendo, em caso de divergência, a questão resolvida segundo as regras da boa fé.
2 – Qualquer dos autores pode, sem prejuízo da exploração em comum de obra feita em colaboração, exercer individualmente os direitos relativos à sua contribuição pessoal, quando esta possa discriminar-se.

Art. 17
Collaborative work

1 – The copyright in a collaborative work, in its entirety, belongs to all that took part in its elaboration and the rules on common property are applicable to the common exercise of copyright.
2 – Unless otherwise agreed in writing, the collaborator's contributions are presumed equal.
3 – If the collaborative work is disclosed or published under the name of only one or some of the collaborators it is presumed, unless otherwise stated, that the remainder have given up their rights to the ones under whose name the work is published or disclosed.
(…)

Art. 18
Individual rights of the authors of the collaborative work

1 – Any of the authors can demand the disclosure, publication, exploitation or modification of the collaborative work and, in case of divergence, the dispute shall be settled according to the rules of good faith.
2 – Any of the authors can, without prejudice to the joint exploitation of the collaborative work, exercise his own individual rights in the contribution inasmuch it is distinguishable.

Artigo 19.º
Obra colectiva

1 – O direito de autor sobre obra colectiva é atribuído à entidade singular ou colectiva que tiver organizado e dirigido a sua criação e em nome de quem tiver sido divulgada ou publicada.

2 – Se, porém, no conjunto da obra colectiva for possível discriminar a produção pessoal de algum ou alguns colaboradores, aplicar-se-á, relativamente aos direitos sobre essa produção pessoal, o preceituado quanto à obra feita em colaboração.

3 – Os jornais e outras publicações periódicas presumem-se obras colectivas, pertencendo às respectivas empresas o direito de autor sobre as mesmas.

Artigo 20.º
Obra compósita

1 – Considera-se obra compósita aquela em que se incorpora, no todo ou em parte, uma obra preexistente, com autorização, mas sem a colaboração do autor desta.

2 – Ao autor de obra compósita pertencem exclusivamente os direitos relativos à mesma, sem prejuízo dos direitos do autor da obra preexistente.

Artigo 165.º
Direitos do autor de obra fotográfica

(…)

2 – Se a fotografia for efectuada em execução de um contrato de trabalho ou por encomenda, presume-se que o direito previsto neste artigo pertence à entidade patronal ou à pessoa que fez a encomenda.

3 – Aquele que utilizar para fins comerciais a reprodução fotográfica

Art. 19
Collective work

1 – The copyright in a collective work is attributed to the natural or legal person that has organized and directed its creation and in whose name it has been disclosed or published.

2 – If, however, in the collective work, it is possible to distinguish the individual contribution of any of the collaborators, the rules on collaborative works are applicable.

3 – Newspapers and other periodic publications are presumed to be collective works, and the copyright on these belongs to the respective companies

Art. 20
Composite work

1 – It is considered to be a composite work, that in which a pre-existing work is incorporated with the authorization but without the collaboration of its author.

2 – The author of a composite work is the sole owner of copyright in it, without prejudice to the copyright in the pre-existing work.

Art 165
Right of the author of a photographic work

(…)

2 – If the photograph is taken in the context of employment or was commissioned, it is presumed that the copyright is owned by the employer or the commissioner.

3 – The one that uses the photographic work for commercial purposes shall pay the author equitable remuneration.

| deve pagar ao autor uma remuneração equitativa. | |

Greek Copyright Act[399]

Article 8: Employee – Created Works

Where a work is created by an employee in the execution of an employment contract the initial holder of the economic and moral rights in the work shall be the author of the work. Unless provided otherwise by contract, only such economic rights as are necessary for the fulfilment of the purpose of the contract shall be transferred exclusively to the employer.

The economic right on works created by employees under any work relation of the public sector or a legal entity of public law in execution of their duties is ipso jure transferred to the employer, unless provided otherwise by contract.

Dutch Copyright Act[400]

Article 5

1. If a literary, scientific if artistic work consists of separate works by two or more persons, the person under whose direction and supervision the work as a whole was made or, if there is no such person, the compiler of the various works, is taken to be the maker of the whole work, without prejudice to the copyright in each of the separate works.

2. Where a separate work in which copyright subsists is incorporated in a whole work, the reproduction or communication to the public of any such separate work by any person other that its maker or his successor in title is regarded as infringement of the copyright in the whole work.

---

399 Law 2121/1993 Copyright, Related Rights and Cultural Matters (Official Journal A 25 1993) , extracted from the Hellenic Intellectual Property Office's website <http://web.opi.gr/xres/p/EN/web.opi.gr/portal/page/portal/opi/info/law2121.html> Acessed 02 September 2013.

400 This is taken from Mireille Van Eechoud, 'Copyright Act – *Auterswet* Unofficial translation in B Hugenholtz, A Quaedvlieg and D Visser (eds) *A Century of Dutch Copyright Law* (deLex 2012) 505.

3. Unless otherwise agreed between the parties, if such a separate work has not previously been made public, the reproduction or making public of that separate work by its maker or his successor in title is regarded as an infringement of the copyright in the whole work of which it is part.

Article 7

Where labour which is carried out in the service of another consists in the making of certain literary, scientific or artistic works, the person in whose service the works were created is taken to be the maker, unless the parties have agreed otherwise.

Article 8

A public institution, an association, a foundation or a company that makes a work public as its own, without naming any natural person as the maker, is taken to be the maker of that work, unless it is proved that in the circumstances the making public of the work was unlawful.

First Proposal for a Council Directive on the legal protection of databases COM (92) 24 final, 13 May 1992

Art. 2
(...)
(5) Member States shall provide for a right for the maker of a database to prevent the unauthorized extraction or re-utilization, from that database, of its contents, in whole or in substantial part, for commercial purposes. This right to prevent unfair extraction of the contents of a database shall apply irrespective of the eligibility of that database for protection under copyright. It shall not apply to the contents of a database where these are works already protected by copyright or neighbouring rights.

Art. 3
(...)
(4) Where a database is created by an employee in the execution of his duties or following the instructions given by his employer, the employer exclusively shall be entitled to exercise all economic rights in the database so created, unless otherwise provided by contract.

Annex II: Selected Legislative Provisions

European Copyright Code[401]

Art. 2.5 – Works made in the course of employment

Unless otherwise agreed, the economic rights in a work created by the author in the execution of his duties or following instructions given by his employer are deemed to be assigned to the employer.

Art. 2.6 – Works made on commission

Unless otherwise agreed, the use of a work by the commissioner of that work is authorised to the extent necessary to achieve the purposes for which the commission was evidently made.

---

401 On the project see B Hugenholtz, 'The Wittem Group's European Copyright Code' in T-E Synodinou (ed), Codification of European Copyright Law (Kluwer Law 2012) 339; J Ginsburg, 'European Copyright Code – Back to First Principles (with Some Additional Detail) ' (2011) Columbia Public Law Research Paper No. 11-261.<http://ssrn.com/abstract=1747148> Acessed 02 September 2013.

Bibliography

Books

Andrews N, *Contract Law* (CUP 2011)
Austen-Baker R, *Implied Terms in English Contract Law* (EE 2011)
Bertani M, *Diritto d'autore europeo* (G. Giapichelli Editore, 2011)
Bertrand A, *Droit d'auteur* (3rd edn, Dalloz 2010)
Canaris C-W, *Die Festellung von Lücken im Gesetz* (2nd edn, Duncker & Humblot 1983)
Chabaud G, *Le Droit d'auteur des Artistes & des Fabricants* (Gazette du Palais 1908)
Clark R, Smyth S and Hall N, *Intellectual Property in Ireland* (3rd edn, Bloomsbury 2010)
Cohen Jehoram T et al, *European Trademark Law* (Kluwer Law 2010)
Cornish W, Llewlyn D and Aplin T, *Intellectual Property: Patents, Copyright, Trade Marks and Allied Rights* (7th edn, Sweet & Maxwell 2010)
Derclaye E and Leistner M, *Intellectual Property Overlaps* (Hart Pub 2011)
Drai L, *Le Droit du Travail Intellectuel* (LGDJ 2005)
Dreier T and Hugenholtz B (eds), *Concise European Copyright Law* (Wolters Kluwer 2006)
Dreier T and Schulze G, *UrhG Kommentar* (4th edn, C.H. Beck 2013)
Fabio P, *Disegni e Modelli* (Cedam 2011)
Ferreti A, *Diritto d'Autore* (Simone 2008)
Fhima I S, *Trade mark dilution in Europe and the United States* (OUP 2011)
Garnett K, Davies G and Harbottle G, *Copinger and Skone James on Copyright* vol I (16th edn, Sweet & Maxwell 2011)
Gervais D (ed), *Collective Management of Copyright and Related Rights* (2nd edn, Kluwer 2010)
Gielen C and Bombhard V (eds), *Concise European trade mark and design law* (Wolters Kluwer 2011)
Goldstein P and Hugenholtz B, *International Copyright: Principles, Law, and Practice* (2nd edn, OUP 2010)
Greffe and Greffe, *Traité des dessins et des modèles*, (8th edn, Lexis Nexis 2008)
Hacon R and Pagenberg J (eds), *Concise European Patent Law* (2 edn, Wolters Kluwer 2009)
Hart H, *The concept of law* (3rd edn, OUP 2012)
Hartlieb and Schwarz, *Handbuch des Film-, Fernseh- und Videorechts* (5th edn, C.H.Beck 2011)
Heller M, *The Gridlock Economy: How Too Much Ownership Wrecks Markets, Stops Innovation, and Costs Lives* (Basic Books 2010)

Bibliography

Holland J and Webb J, *Learning Legal Rules* (7th edn, OUP 2010)
Jankowski J, *Markenschutz für Kunstwerke* (Nomos 2012)
Kamina P, *Film Copyright in the European Union* (CUP 2002)
Köhler H, *BGB Allgemeiner Teil* (35th edn, C.H. Beck 2011)
Kolasa M, *The Scope and Limits of Protection for Distinctive Signs against the Community Design* (Nomos 2012)
Kraßer R, *Patentrecht* (6th edn, C.H.Beck 2009)
Kur A and Dreier T, *European Intellectual Property Law – Text, Cases & Materials* (EE 2013)
Laddie, Prescott and Vitoria, The modern law of copyright and designs, (4th edn, Lexis Nexis Butterworths 2011)
Larenz K, *Methodenlehre der Rechtswissenschaft* (6th edn, Springer 1991)
Leistner M, D*er Rechtsschutz von Datenbaken im deutschen und europäischen Recht* (C.H. Beck 2000)
Lewinski S V, *International Copyright Law and Policy* (OUP 2008)
– (ed), *Intellectual Property & Indigenous Heritage* (2nd edn, Kluwer 2008)
Loewenheim U, *Handbuch des Urheberrechts* (2nd edn, C.H. Beck 2010)
Lucas and Lucas, *Traité de la propriété littéraire et artistique* (4th edn, Lexis Nexis 2012)
Lucas-Schloetter A, *Les droits d'auteur des salariés en Europe continentale* (Cahiers IRPI 2004)
Luhmann N, *Law as a Social System* (OUP 2004)
MacCormick N, *Rhetoric and the Rule of Law – A theory of Legal Reasoning* (OUP 2005)
Manthey A, *Die Filmrechtsregelungen in den wichtigsten filmproduzierenden Ländern Europas und den USA* (Nomos 1993)
Martin J-P, *Droit des inventions de salariés* (3rd edn Lexis Nexis 2005)
Miller R et al, *Terrel on the Law of Patents* (17th edn, Sweet & Maxwell 2010)
Pouillet E, *Traité théorique et pratique de propriété littéraire et artistique et du droit de representation* (Paris 1908)
Ricketson S and Ginsburg, J *International Copyright and Neighbouring Rights* vol 2 (2nd edn, OUP 2006)
Rosati E, *Originality in EU Copyright – Full Harmonization through Case Law* (EE 2013)
Ruhl O, *Gemeinshcaftsgeschamcksmuster Kommentar* (2nd edn, Carl Heymanns 2010)
de Sanctis V M, *I soggetti del dirrito d'autore* (Giuffré 2005)
– –, *Manuale del Nuovo Diritto d'autore* (Scientifica 2010)
Schwarz C and Kruspig S, *Computerimplementierte Erfindungen – Patentschutz von Software?* (Carl Heymanns 2011)
Schricker G and Loewenheim U, *Urheberrecht Kommentar* (4th edn C.H. Beck 2010)
Seignette J, *Challenges to the creator doctrine* (Wolters Kluwer 1994).
Senftleben M, *Copyright, Limitations and the Three-step Test* (Kluwer Law International 2004).

Steinke T, *Die Verwirkung im Immaterialgüterrecht* (V&R unipress 2006)
Sterling J, *World Copyright law* (3rd edn, Sweet and Maxwell 2008)
Strowel A, *Droit d'auteur et copyright* (Brulyant 1993)
Stier P M, *Laches und equitable estoppel im U.S.-amerkinaschinen und Verwirkung im deutschen Patent- und Urheberrecht* (Carl Heymanns 2004)
Stone D, *European Union Design Law* (OUP 2012)
Tomkowicz R, *Intellectual Property Overlaps* (Routledge 2011)
Trimborn M, *Employees Inventions in Germany: A Handbook for International Business* (Wolters Kluwer 2009)
Tsoutsanis A, *Trade mark registrations in bad faith* (OUP 2010).
Ulmer E, *Urheber- und Verlagsrecht* (3rd edn, Springer 1980)
Vanzetti and Di Cataldo, *Manuale di Diritto Industriale* (7th edn, Giuffré 2012)
Vivant M and Navarro J, *Code de la propriété intellectuelle* (Lexis nexis 2013)
Walter M and Lewinski S V (eds), *European Copyright Law* (OUP 2010)

Articles and Contributions to edited books

Anonymous 'Note: A justification for allowing fragmentation in copyright' [2011] HLR 1751
Aarab K, 'Droit d'auteur et droit des dessins et modèles : le conflit de la recevabilité à agir des personnes morales' 68 (2011) Revue Lamy Droit de l'immatériel 97
Amor D, 'Protecting Italian Lamps and Egg Chairs: Proposed Repeal of Section 52 CDPA (UK)' 26 (2010) WIPR 30
Angelopoulos C, 'The Myth of European Term Harmonisation: 27 Public Domains for the 27 Member States' [2012] IIC 567
Bayreuther F, 'Zum Verhältnis zwischen Arbeits-, Urheber- und Arbeitnehmererfindugsrecht Unter besonderer Berücksichtigung der Sondervergütungansprüche des angestellten Softwareerstellers' [2003] GRUR 570
Bently L, 'Interpretation of Copyright Rules: The Role of the Interpreter – the Creation Function' available at <http://www.cipil.law.cam.ac.uk/Judicial%20Creativity%20in%20Copyright%20Interpretation.pdf> accessed 31 August 2013
– –, 'The return of industrial copyright' [2012] EIPR 654
Briges A, 'Navigating the interface between utility patents and copyrights' in N Wilkof and S Basheer (eds) *Overlapping Intellectual Property Rights* (OUP 2012) 1
Calabresi G and Melamed A, 'Property rules, liability rules, and inalienability: one view of the cathedral' [1982] HLR 1089
de Carvalho N P, 'Towards a Unified Theory of Intellectual Property: The Differentiating Capacity (and Function) as the Thread That Unites All its Components [2012] JWIP 251
Chalton S, 'The Copyright and Rights in Databases Regulations 1997: some outstanding issues on implementation of the Database Directive' [1998] EIPR 178

Bibliography

Christie A and Dent C, 'Non-overlapping rights: a patent misconception' [2010] EIPR 58

Cohen Jehoram T, 'The Function Theory in European Trade Mark Law and the Holistic Approach of the CJEU' (2012) 102 The Trademark Reporter 1243

Cook T, 'How IPrs, like Nature, Abhor a Vacuum, and What Can Happen When They Fill it – Lacunae and Overlaps in Intellectual Property' (2012) 17 JIPR 296

Cookson B E, 'The significance of goodwill' EIPR [1991] 248.

Cornish W, 'The expansion of Intellectual Property Rights' in Schricker, Dreier and Kur (eds) *Geistiges Eigentum im Dienst der Innovation* (Nomos 2001) 9.

Cornwell J, 'Dyson and Samsung Compared: Functionality and Aestethics in the Design Infringement Analysis' [2013] EIPR 273

Davidson M and Hugenholtz B, 'Football fixtures, horse races and spin-offs: the ECJ domesticates the database right' [2005] EIPR 113.

Davies J and Durant A, 'To protect or not to protect? The eligibility of commercially-used short verbal texts for copyright and trade mark protection' [2011] IPQ 345

Derclaye E, 'La Belgique: un pays de cocagne pour les créateurs de dessins et modèles' 14.2 (2009) *Intellectuel rechten- Droits intellectuels* 100

Dinwoodie G, 'Trademark And Copyright: Complements or Competitors?' in J Ginsburg and J Besek (eds), *Adjuncts and Alternatives to Copyright* (ALAI-USA 2002) 506

– –,, 'Concurrence and Convergence of Rights: The concerns of the US Supreme Court in Intellectual Property Law' in W Grosheide and J Brinkhof (eds), *Articles on Crossing Borders between traditional and actual Intellectual Property Law* (Intersentia 2004) 5

– –, 'Trademarks and Territory: Detaching Trademark Law from the Nation-State' (2004) 41 Houston Law Review 886

Dietz A, 'The Concept of Author under the Berne Convention' 155 (1993) RIDA 2

– –, 'Das Urhebervertragsrecht in seiner rechtpolitischen Bedeutung' in F-K Beier et al. (eds) *Urhebervertragsrecht* (C.H. Beck 1995) 1

Dreier T, 'The Council Directive of 14 May 1991 on the Legal Protection of Computer Programs' [1991] EIPR 319

Du Mont J and Janis M, ' Functionality in Design Protection Systems' (2012) 19 Journal of Intellectual Property Law 261.

Dworkin R, 'On Gaps in the Law' in P Amselek and N MacCormick (eds), *Controversies about Law's Ontology* (Edinburgh University Press 1991) 84

Eechoud M V, 'Copyright Act – *Auterswet* Unofficial translation in B Hugenholtz, A Quaedvlieg and D Visser (eds) *A Century of Dutch Copyright Law* (deLex 2012) 505.

– –, 'Along the Road to Uniformity – Diverse Readings of the Court of Justice Judgments on Copyright Work' [2012] JIPITEC 60.

Fhima I S, 'How Does 'Essential Function' Doctrine Drive European Trade Mark Law?' [2005] IIC 401.

Fuchs T, 'Der Arbeitnehmerurheber im System des § 43 UrhG' [2006] GRUR 561

Gaide A-V, 'Copyright, Trademarks and Trade Dress: Overlap or Conflict for Cartoon Characters?' in J Ginsburg and J Besek (eds) (n 5) 552

Galloux J-C, 'Des possibles cumuls de protection par les droits de propriété intellectuelle' in *L'entreprise face à la contrefaçon des droits de propriété intellectuelle* (Litec 2002) 81

Gaubiac Y, 'La théorie de l'unité de l'art' 111 (1982) RIDA 3

Gaudrat P, 'Les démêlés intemporels d'un couple à succès: le créateur et l'investisseur' 190 (2001) RIDA 71

Gendreau Y, 'Le critère de fixation en droit d'auteur' 159 (1994) RIDA 111

Ginsburg J, 'A Tale of Two Copyrights: Literary Property in Revolutionary France and America' [1990] Tulane Law Review 991
 – –, The concept of authorship (2002) 52 Depaul Law Review 1063

Ghidini G, 'From here to eternity? On the overlap of shape trade marks with design protection' in J Drexl, R Hilty, L Boy and C Godt (eds), *Technology and Competition. Contributions in Honour of Hanns Ullrich* 55

Graef R, 'Die fiktive Figur im Urheberrecht' [2012] ZUM 108

Golder T and Mayer A, 'Whose IP is it anyway?' [2009] JIPLP 165

Gompel S V and Lavik E, 'Quality, Merit, Aesthetics and Purpose: An inquiry into EU Copyright law's eschewal of other criteria than originality' 236 (2013) RIDA 100.

Götting H-P, 'Urheberrechtliche und vertagsrechtliche Grundlagen' in F-K Beier et al. (eds) (n 268) 53, 72
 – –, 'Der Begriff des Geistigen Eigentums' [2005] GRUR 353

Hartwig H, 'the Court of Justice: "Seated Figure"' [2013] IIC 248
 – –, 'Unregistered and registered Community design rights: further guidance expected from CJEU' [2013] JIPLP 241
 – –, 'Unzulässige Werbeabbildung eines Geschmacksmusters zu Zitatzwecken' [2011] GRUR 1117

Heller M, 'The tragedy of the anticommons: property in the transition from Marx to markets' [1998] HLR 621
 – – and Eisenberg R, 'Can Patents Deter Innovation? The Anticommons in Biomedical Research' Science 280 (1998) 698

Hilty R and Geiger C, 'Towards a New Instrument of Protection for Software in the EU? Learning the Lessons from the Harmonization Failure of Software Patentability' in E Arezzo and G Ghidini (eds) *Biotechnology And Software Patent Law* (EE 2011) 153.

Hugenholtz B, 'The Wittem Group's European Copyright Code' in T-E Synodinou (ed), Codification of European Copyright Law (Kluwer Law 2012) 339

Hunter D, 'Reason is too large: Analogy and precedent in law' 50 Emory Law Journal (2001) 1197

Jones M, Licensee Estoppel: an overview of the position under English and European law in [2007] JIPLP 750

Katzenberger P, 'Protection of the Author as the Weaker Party to a Contract under International Copyright Contract Law' [1988] IIC 731

Klink J, 'Titles in Europe' [2004] EIPR 290

Kraßer R, 'Urheberrecht in Arbeits-, Dienst- und Auftragsverhältnissen' in F-K Beier et al. (eds) (n 268) 77.

Bibliography

Kur A, 'The "Presentation Right" – Time to Create a New Limitation in Copyright Law?' [2000] IIC 308

– –, 'Exceptions to Protection Where Copyright and Trade Mark Overlap' in J Ginsburg and J Besek (eds), *Adjuncts and Alternatives to Copyright* (ALAI-USA 2002) 594

– –, 'Cumulation of IP Rights Pertaining to Product Shapes. An "Illegitimate Offspring" of IP Law?' in G Ghidini and L Genovesi (eds), *Intellectual Property and Market Power* (Eudeba 2008) 613

– –, 'Too Pretty to Protect? Trade Mark Law and the Enigma of Aesthetic Functionality' in J Drexl, R Hilty, L Boy and C Godt (eds), *Technology and Competition. Contributions in Honour of Hanns Ullrich* 139

Langenbucher K, 'Argument by Analogy in European Law' 57 (2008) Cambridge Law Journal 481

Le Stanc C, 'Interférences entre droit d'auteur et droit de brevet quant a la protection du logiciel: approche française' in S K Verma and R Mittal (eds), *IPRs A global vision* 162

Leistner M, 'The protection of databases' in E Derclaye (ed), *Research Handbook on the Future of EU Copyright* (EE 2009) 427

– –, 'Der europäisches Werkbegriff' [2013] ZGE 4

– –,'Book Review – Till Kreutzer, Das Modell des deutschen Urheberrechts und Regelungslasternativen' [2011] JIPITEC 165

Lenaerts A, 'The General Principle of the Prohibition of Abuse of Rights: A Critical Position on Its Role in a Codified European Contract Law' 6 (2010) ERPL 1121.

Lewinski S V, 'Collectivism and its role in the frame of individual contracts' in in J Rosén (ed) *Individualism and Collectiveness in Intellectual Property Law* (EE 2012) 117

Macrez F, 'Cumuls de Droits Intellectuels sur les créations informatiques' in A Cruquenaire and S Dusollier (eds), *Le Cumul des Droits Intellectuels* (Larcier 2009) 87.

Marchese D, 'Joint ownership of intellectual property' [1999] EIPR 364

Margoni T and Perry M, 'Ownership in complex authorship: a comparative study of joint works in copyright law' [2012] EIPR 22

Maris C W, 'Milking the Meter.' in P Nerhot (ed), *Legal Knowledge and Analogy* (Springer1991) 71

Massa C-H and Strowel A, 'Community Design: Cinderella revamped' [2003] EIPR 68, – – and Strowel A, 'Le cumul du dessin ou modèle et du droit d'auteur : orbites parallèles et forces d'attraction entre deux planètes indépendantes mais jumelles' in A Cruquenaire and S Dusollier (eds), *Le Cumul des Droits Intellectuels* (Larcier 2009) 21

McIntyre T J, 'Copyright in custom code: Who owns commissioned software?' [2007] JIPLP 473

Mende C and Isaac B, 'When copyright and trademark rights overlap' in Wilkof N and Basheer S (eds), *Overlapping Intellectual Property Rights* (OUP 2012) 137

Metzger A, 'Vom Einzelurheber zu Teams und Netzwerken: Erosion des Schöpferprinzips?' in S Leible, A Ohly and H Zech (eds), *Wissen – Markte – Geistiges Eigentum* 79
– –,'Abuse of Law in EC Private Law: A (re-)construction from fragments' in R de La Feria and S Vogenauer (eds), *Prohibition of Abuse of Law: A New General Principle in EC Law?* (Hart Publishing 2010) 235
Miller C G, 'Magill: Time to abandond the "specific subject matter" concept' [1993] EIPR 415
Moffat V R, 'Mutant Copyrights and Backdoor Patents: the Problem of Overlapping Intellectual Property Protection' (2004) 19 Berkeley Technology Law Journal 1473
Ohly A, 'Geistiges Eigentum?' [2003] JZ 545.
– –, 'Choice of Law in the Digital Environment – Problems and Possible Solutions' in J Drexl and A Kur (eds) *Intellectual Property and Private International Law* (Hart Publishing 2005)
– –, 'Areas of Overlap Between Trade Mark Rights, Copyright and Design Rights in German Law' [2007] GRUR Int 704
Overwalle G V, 'Individualism, collectivism and openness in patent law: from exclusion to inclusion through licensing' in J Rosén, *Individualism and Collectiveness in Intellectual Property Law* (EE 2012) 71
Peukert A, 'Individual multiple and collective ownership of intellectual property rights – which impact on exclusivitiy?' in A Kur and V Mizaras (eds) *The Structure of Intellectual Property Law: Can One Size Fit All?* (EE 2011) 195
Pihlajarinne T, 'Setting the limits for the implied license in copyright and linking discourse – the European perspective' [2012] IIC 700
Pila J, 'Sewing the Fly Buttons on the Statute' Employee Inventions and the Employment Context' 32 (2012) OJLS 265
Quaedvlieg, A 'Concurrence and Convergence in Industrial Design: 3-Dimensional Shapes Excluded by Trademark Law' in W Grosheide and J Brinkhof (eds), *Articles on Crossing Borders between traditional and actual Intellectual Property Law* (Intersentia 2004) 23
– –, 'Overlap/relationships between copyright and other intellectual property rights' in E Derclaye (ed), *Research Handbook on the Future of EU Copyright* (EE 2009) 480,
– –, 'Authorship and Ownership: Authors, Entrepeneurs and Rights' in T-E Synodinou (ed), Codification of European Copyright Law (Kluwer Law 2012) 197
Rahmatian A, 'Dealing with rights in copyright-protected works: assignment and licences' in E Derclaye (ed), *Research Handbook on the Future of EU Copyright* (EE 2009) 286
– –, 'Intellectual Property and the Concept of Dematerialised Property in S Bright (ed) *Modern Studies in Property Law* vol 6 (Hart Publishing 2011) 361
– –, 'Originality in UK Copyright Law: The Old "Skill and Labour" Doctrine Under Pressure [2013] IIC 4.
Reeskamp P, 'Dr No in trade mark country: a Dutch point of view' [2010] JIPLP 29.

Bibliography

Ricketson S and Suthersanen U, 'The design/copyright overlap: is there a resolution?' in Wilkof N and Basheer S (eds), *Overlapping Intellectual Property Rights* (OUP 2012) 159

Ricolfi M, Collective Rights Management in a Digital Environment in in G Ghidini and L Genovesi (eds), Intellectual Property and Market Power (Eudeba 2008) 383

Rocha M V, 'A titularidade das criações intelectuais no âmbito da relação de trabalho' in *Nos 20 anos do Código das Sociedades Comerciais* (Coimbra Ed 2007)

Rognstad O-A, 'The multiplicity of territorial IP rights and its impact on competition' in J Rosén (ed) *Individualism and Collectiveness in Intellectual Property Law* (EE 2012) 55

Sanders A K, '100 years of copyright – The Interface with design law coming full circle?' in B Hugenholtz, A Quaedvlieg and D Visser (eds) (n92) 99

Savitsky P, 'Protection of product appearance in Russia' [2013] EIPR 143

Seignette J, 'Authorship, Copyright Ownership and Works made on Commission and under Employment' in B Hugenholtz, A Quaedvlieg and D Visser (eds) *A Century of Dutch Copyright Law* (deLex 2012) 115

Senftleben M, 'Overprotection and Protection Overlaps in Intellectual Property Law – the Need for Horizontal Fair Use Defences' in A Kur and V Mizaras (eds), *The Structure of Intellectual Property Law: Can One Size Fit All?* (EE 2011)

– –,'Der Kulturelle Imperativ des Urheberrechts' in M Weller, N Kemle, T Dreier and M Lynen (eds), *Kunst im Markt – Kunst im Recht* (Nomos 2010) 75

Sousa e Silva N, 'No copyright protection for tap designs – says Portuguese Court' [2013] JIPLP 686.

– –, 'Novelty is not enough: Spanish Supreme Court rejects unity of the art in an enigmatic decision' [2013] JIPLP 825

Shapiro C, 'Navigating the Patent Thicket: Cross Licenses, Patent Pools, and Standard-Setting' in A Jaffe, J Lerner and S Stern (eds), *Innovation Policy and the Economy* vol 1 (MIT Press 2001) 119.

Spindler G, 'Miturhebergemeinschaft und BGB-Gesellschaft' in A Ohly et al (eds), *Perspektiven des Geistiges Eigentums und Wettbewerbsrecht – Festschrift für Gerhard Schricker zum 70. Geburtstag* (C.H. Beck 2005).

Strowel A and Vanbrabant B, 'Copyright licensing: a European view' in J de Werra (ed) *Research Handbook on Intellectual Property Licensing* (EE 2013) 29

Torremans P, 'Choice of law in EU copyright directives' in E Derclaye (ed), *Research Handbook on the Future of EU Copyright* (EE 2009) 457

Ubertazzi L C, 'Spunti sulla comunione in diritto d'autore' [2003] AIDA 506

Verkade F, 'The cumulative Effect of Copyright Law and Trademark Law: Which takes precedence?' in J Kabel and G Mom (eds) Intellectual Property and Information Law: Essays in Honour of Herman Cohen Jehoram (Kluwer Law 1998) 69.

Voon T and Mitchell A, 'Implications of WTO Law for Plain Packaging of Tobacco Products' in A. Mitchell, T. Voon and J. Liberman (eds), *Public Health and Plain Packaging of Cigarettes: Legal Issues* (EE 2012) 109

Waisman A, 'May authorship go objective?' [2009] JIPLP 583

Wandtke A and Bullinger W, 'Die Marke als urheberrechtlich schutzfähiges Werk' [1997] GRUR 573

Weil P, 'The Court Cannot Conclude Definitively...Non Liquet Revisited' (1997) 36 Columbia Journal of Transnational Law 109

Wernick A S, 'The work for hire and joint work copyright doctrines after CCNV V. REID: "What! You mean I don't own it even though I paid in full for it?"' (1990) 13 Hamline Law Review 287

Whittaker S and Zimmerman R, 'Coming to terms with good faith' in S Whittaker and R Zimmerman (eds) *Good faith in European contract law* (CUP 2000) 654

– –, 'Good faith in European contract law: surveying the legal landscape' in S Whittaker and R Zimmerman (eds) *Good faith in European contract law* (CUP 2000) 46

Wolk S, 'Remuneration of Employee Inventors – Is there a Common European Ground? A comparison of National laws on Compensation of Inventors in Germany, France, Spain, Sweden and the United Kingdom' [2011] IIC 272

– –, 'EU Intellectual Property Law and Ownership in Employment Relationships' in *Information & Communication Technology, Legal Issues, Scandinavian Studies in Law* (Wahlgren 2010) 419.

Zermer L, 'Contribution and collaboration in joint authorship: too many misconceptions' [2006] JIPLP 283

Zografos D, 'Tradition v Trade marks: The New Zealand Trade Marks Act 2002' in W Grosheide and J Brinkhof (eds), *Articles on Crossing Borders between traditional and actual Intellectual Property Law* (Intersentia 2004) 279

Research papers

Ginsburg J, 'European Copyright Code – Back to First Principles (with Some Additional Detail)' (2011); Columbia Public Law Research Paper No. 11-261.<http://ssrn.com/abstract=1747148> Acessed 02 September 2013

Kur A and Grosse Ruse–Khan H, 'Enough is Enough – The Notion of Binding Ceilings in International Intellectual Property Protection' (2008) Max Planck Institute for Intellectual Property, Competition & Tax Law Research Paper Series No. 09-01, 8 <http://ssrn.com/abstract=1326429> accessed 16 August 2013

Moufang R, 'The interface between patents and plant variety rights in Europe' (WIPO-UPOV/SYM/03/06)

Schauer F, 'Why Precedent in Law (and Elsewhere) is Not Totally (or Even Substantially) about Analogy' KSG Working Paper No. RWP07-036 (2007) <http://ssrn.com/abstract=1747148> accessed 02 January 2014.

Bibliography

Official documents and other materials

AIPPI summary report to question Q194 "The Impact of Co-Ownership of Intellectual Property Rights on their Exploitation" available at <https://www.aippi.org/download/commitees/194/SR194English.pdf> accessed 28 August 2013

Commission, 'Staff Working Paper on the Review of the EC Legal Framework in the field of copyright' SEC(2004)995

Guibault L and Hugenholtz B, *Study on the Conditions Applicable to Contracts Relating to Intellectual Property in the European Union* (Final Report) (study no ETD/2000 / B5-3001/E/69)

Guidelines for Examination in the European Patent Office (20 June 2012), available at <http://www.epo.org/law-practice/legal-texts/guidelines.html> accessed 25 August 2013

Max Planck Institute, 'Study on the Overall Functioning of the European Trade Mark System' available at <http://ec.europa.eu/internal_market/indprop/docs/tm/20110308_allensbach-study_en.pdf> accessed 30 October 2013

OHIM Manual of Trade Mark Practice, available at <http://oami.europa.eu/ows/rw/pages/CTM/legalReferences/guidelines/OHIMManual.en.do> accessed 12 August 2013

Resolution of the Plenum of the Supreme Court of the Russian Federation and the Supreme Commercial Court of the Russian Federation No. 5/29 of March 26, 2009 "On Certain Questions Arising in Relation to the Enactment of the Fourth Part of the Civil Code of the Russian Federation."

UN Committee on Economic, Social and Cultural Rights (CESCR), *General Comment No. 17: The Right of Everyone to Benefit from the Protection of the Moral and Material Interests Resulting from any Scientific, Literary or Artistic Production of Which He or She is the Author (Art. 15, Para. 1 (c) of the Covenant)* (12 January 2006) E/C.12/GC/17, 3 available at: <http://www.refworld.org/docid/441543594.html> accessed 24 August 2013.

Cases

Court of Justice of the European Union[402]

C-479/12, *Gautzsch Großhandel* (pending)

C-320/12 *Malaysia* (CJEU 27 June 2013)

C-101/11 P and C-102/11 P *Herbert Neuman and Others v José Manuel Baena Grupo SA* (CJEU 18 October 2012)

C-406/10 *SAS Institute Inc. v World Programming Ltd* (CJEU 2 May 2012)

C-277/10 *Martin Luksan v Petrus van der Let* (CJEU 9 February 2012)

---

402 Formerly European Court of Justice.

C-393/09 *Bezpečnostní softwarová asociace* (BSA) [2010] ECR I-13971
C-168/09 *Flos v Semeraro* [2011] ECR I-181
C-403/08 and C-429/08 *Football Dataco* (CJEU 4 October 2011)
C-398/08 P Audi AG v OHIM [2010] ECR I-535
C-32/08 *FEIA v Cul de Sac* [2009] ECR I-5611.
C-5/08 *Infopaq International A/S v Danske Dagblades Forening* [2009] ECR I-6569
C-529/07 *Lindt* [2009] ECR I-04893
C-487/07 *L'Oréal v Bellure* [2009] ETMR 55
C-304/07 *Directmedia Publishing GmbH v Albert-Ludwigs-Universität Freiburg* [2008] ECR I-7565
C-28/04 *Tod's* [2005] ECR I-5781
C-353/03 *Société des produits Nestlé SA v Mars UK Ltd* [2005] ECR I-6135
C-203/02 *BHB v William Hill* [2004] ECR I-10415
C-414/99 to C-416/99 *Zino Davidoff* [2001] ECR I-8691
C-337/95 *Parfums Christian Dior SA* [1997] ECR I-06013
C-92/92 and C-326/92 *Phill Collins* [1993] ECR I-5145
Case 30/88 *Hellenic Republic v Commission* [1989] ECR I-3711
78/70 *Deutsche Grammophon* [1971] ECR 487

General Court[403]

Case T-666/11 *Danuta Budziewska v OHIM – Puma* (GC 7 November 2013) (only available in French and Polish)
T-608/11 *Beifa Group II* (GC 27 June 2013)
T-68/11 *Erich Kastenholz v OHIM* (GC 6 June 2013)
T-579/10 *macros* (GC 7 May 2013)
T-55/12 *Su-Shan Chen* (GC 25 April 2013)
T-148/08 *Beifa Group v OHIM – Schwan-Stabilo Schwanhäußer (Instrument d'écriture)* [2010] ECR II–1681
T-435/05 *Danjaq v OHMI – Mission Productions (Dr. No)* [2009] ECR II–2097

OHIM

Case ICD 8721, Invalidity Division 14 May 2013
Decisions of the cancellation division of 15 November 2012, 3555C and 3556C
BoA decision of 6 July 2005 R869/2004-1 *Gallo Winery*

EPO

Opinion of the Enlarged Board of Appeal of 12 May 2010 (G3/08)

---

403 Formerly Court of First Instance.

Bibliography

UK

Lucasfilms Ltd v Ainsworth [2009] EWCA Civ 1328 [163].
Griggs v Evans (II) [2005] 2 WLR 513
Clearsprings Management Ltd -v Businesslink Ltd [2005] EWHC 1487
Bamgboye v Reed [2004] 5 EMLR 61
Griggs v Evans [2003] EWHC 2914
Ray v Classic FM Plc [1998] ECC 488
Warner v Gestetner Ltd [1988] EIPR D89
BP refinery (Westernport) Pty LTd v Shire of Hastings 180 CLR 266 (1977)
e I.R.C. v Muller & Co's Margarine Ltd. [1901] A.C

Germany

BGH [2013] I ZR 143/12 – *Geburtstagzug*
BGH [2012] GRUR 612 *Medusa*
BGH [2011] GRUR 1117 *Deutschebahn v Fraunhofer*
BGH [2011] GRUR 59
Munich Regional Court 13 June 2007, ZUM-RD [2007] 498
BGH [2001] GRUR 155 *Wetterführungspläne*
[1998] GRUR 1021 *Monalisa*
BGH [1995] GRUR 581 *Silberdiestel*
BGH [1992] GRUR 310 *Taschenbuch-Lizenz*
BGH [1991] GRUR 523 *Grabungsmaterialien*

France

French *Cour de cassation* (22 March 2012, appeal no 11-10132)
Petit Robert [2005] RIDA 236.

Spain

Decision 561/2012 (official publication number STS 6196/2012), by the Civil Section of The Spanish Supreme Court, 27 September 2012

Portugal

Process 1607/10.3TBBRG.G1, decision by Guimarães Court of Appeal of 27 February 2012